Buff and Polish

A Practical Guide to Enhance Your Professional Image and Communication Style

DONNA:

A PERSONAL note of
APPECiation For your
continued SUPPOt s
conFidence in me.
Thank you!

Kathryn

Buff and Polish

A Practical Guide to Enhance Your Professional Image and Communication Style

Kathryn J. Volin

Pentagon Publishing
Minneapolis, Minnesota

Although the author and publisher have made every effort to ensure the accuracy and completeness of information contained in this book, we assume no responsibility for errors, inaccuracies, omissions, or any inconsistency herein. Any slights of people, places, or organizations are unintentional.

First printing 1999

ISBN 0-9666878-6-8

LCCN 98-92150

ATTENTION CORPORATIONS, UNIVERSITIES, COLLEGES, AND PROFESSIONAL ORGANIZATIONS: Quantity discounts are available on bulk purchases of this book for educational purposes. Special books or book excerpts can also be created to fit specific needs. For information, please contact Pentagon Publishing, 2626 East 82nd Street; Suite 228, Minneapolis, MN 55425-1381, 651-436-1212.

CONTENTS

ACKNOWLEDGMENTS

This book is dedicated to my incredible husband, Jim, whose ardent support, loving encouragement, and belief in me has been extraordinary. Also, many thanks to my mother, Arlene Rauchwarter, the most dedicated, dependable, and efficient assistant ever!

THANK YOU . . .

- Dad (we miss you) for making me believe I could be successful at *everything.*

- Ann Marie Hines, you are, without a doubt, the greatest sister and best friend I could hope for, and Tom Hines, for being such a wise and wonderful brother-in-law.

- Bonnie Swanson for your superb input and for constantly telling me "You can do it!"

- Christy Goral for caring, sharing, listening, and for being such a great friend.

- Amy Sperry for your sparkling personality, terrific wit, and invaluable suggestions.

- Bob Anderson for your loyalty, boundless energy, and brilliant sense of humor.

- All of the participants of my workshops and the executives I have coached who have taught me so much and supported me so generously.

- My friends, family, and clients who have continued to endorse, inspire, and believe in me: Mike Anderson, Mike Bell, Julie

Bontempo, Bob Cummins, Dan Caspersen, Jim Dahl, Chuck Denny, Dave Eske, Roland Foubert, Alan Giangreco, Bill Goodwin, Lou Grespan, Sharon Gunberg, Phil Heinz, Darla Hines, Steve Kenady, Betty Kimbrough, Scott LaFond, Harold Mulet, David, Dennis, Mary, Steve, and Gretchen Rauchwarter, Dan Schultzetenberg, Michael Stephens, Dennis Stolp, and Carolyn and Chuck Yates.

My venture would not have been as fun, enlightening, and certainly not as exciting without all of you involved. Thanks so much for being a part of it!

INTRODUCTION

Did you know that 55 percent of our believability and the way we are perceived is based on our body language, which includes posture, gestures, and eye contact? Did you know that 38 percent of our believability and the way we are perceived is based on our voice, which includes projection, inflection, and rate? Did you know that only 7 percent of our believability and the way we are perceived is based on our message or the actual information we are providing our listeners? Most of us don't realize it, but people are sizing us up within the first three to four seconds of an encounter. They are making judgments about us at seven seconds, and within thirty seconds they have made at least eleven assumptions about us, including social status, economic status, education, occupation, marital status, ancestry, trustworthiness, credibility, and likelihood to succeed.

Today, in a situation where three people with equal qualifications are interviewed for a job, the one with the best communication skills gets it. The ability to communicate well is ranked the number-one key to success by leaders in business, politics, and the professions. For seven out of ten people who lose their jobs, the reason isn't lack of skill. According to executive recruiters, it's personality conflicts, ego, and poor communication style.

Think about the last time you drove your automobile to the car wash. Do you remember how it looked **before** it was *buffed and polished* and how remarkable it looked **after** the attendants spent time rubbing, scrubbing, and *buffing and polishing* your vehicle? Visualize yourself *buffed and polished*, conveying a professional image and strong communication style. ***Buff and Polish*** is not like most books. It's not a book to read—it's a book to *use*. The simple yet sound techniques and suggestions presented can make a dramatic change in one's ability to achieve excellence while interacting with others.

This book was originally envisioned as a supplement to the Effective Communications Program offered at Communication Concepts International, Inc. Because retention of information has been proven to be approximately 5 percent, I felt it was crucial to provide training reinforcement to enhance the results of our programs. My goal was to furnish our clients with an overview of the information addressed during the program that could be referred to and easily carried in their briefcase or luggage. The result is an abundant collection of the most successful theories and techniques I have compiled and applied over the past twenty years. This knowledge can be used to enhance **anyone's** professional image and overall communication style. My basic philosophy is this: We *all* have the ability to generate positive and effective results in the way we communicate and in the way we are perceived. Sometimes, however, we just don't know *how* to go about it or *where* to begin.

Buff and Polish is a "must read" for virtually everyone in the business world. Whether you are a college graduate, a professional on the rise, or a seasoned executive, achieving excellence in interpersonal communications will ensure your continued personal and professional growth and success. Through the application of specific principles and methods, you will find the opportunities to utilize and maximize your potential are limitless.

Some of the subtle but critical success factors we will address throughout this exceptional book include:

- First impressions and their enormous impact—a personal inventory.
- Confident handshakes and introductions—get a good grip on every situation.

- Professional presence—improve your image, style, and how you are perceived.
- Movement and gestures—actions speak louder than words; gesturing for impact.
- Important elements—eye contact, facial expressions, and body language signals.
- The power of your voice—it's not what you say, it's how you say it.
- Effective listening techniques—increasing your rate of success.
- Handling challenging questions and difficult situations, and thinking on your feet.
- Business etiquette—dining, entertaining, and traveling.
- The art of self-promotion—"blowing your horn" without being obnoxious.
- Making great presentations: preparing, delivering, and holding an audience's interest.

If the person you want to be is someone who is trustworthy, friendly, likable, credible, memorable, impressive, and effective from the very first encounter, then you are reading the right book. I don't want you to think you have to become someone you're not; you don't. You simply must learn to *be yourself, at your best, all the time.* Practice and follow the proven strategies and advice presented in this book to polish your picture of success; you won't be disappointed with the results. **Buff and Polish** will help you realize that you have the ability within you to become a powerful, believable, and successful communicator.

CHAPTER 1

First Impressions

First impressions can be effective or they can be disastrous, but they are forever lasting. Whether you are walking into a room for a job interview, meeting with a new client, or making a presentation, the image you portray is your calling card and is vital to how others perceive you. Believe it or not, people are sizing you up within the first **three to four seconds** of an encounter, they're making judgments about you at **seven seconds**, and within **thirty seconds** they've made at least eleven assumptions about you. These assumptions include social status, economic status, education, occupation, marital status, ancestry, trustworthiness, credibility, and likelihood to succeed.

On the telephone, we have even less time—only **seven seconds**—to make a first impression. Because we are deprived of being able to use our body language and facial expressions to influence people, those seven seconds are critical. The choices you make as you create your own image can, if well chosen, transmit a very positive statement about you and what you think about yourself. We tend to judge a book by its cover and people by their looks and clothes. Keep this in mind: **You never get a second chance to make a first impression**, so make the first one count!

People form their impressions of you by looking at the outside and making assumptions about what's on the inside; they take you at face value. Your physical presence is the foundation on

5

which you build your credibility. Making a positive first impression is not fawning over someone, falsely flattering them, or appearing subordinate and submissive. Your entrance into a room should establish control and presence. Confident people have a rhythm to their movements and an energy to their stride. Appear self-assured and the people you meet will **believe** you to be self-assured. You just have to *be yourself* at your best. No one can play *you* as well as *you* can. The secret to good communications is to be consistently *you, at your best,* in all situations.

In a job interview, approximately 75 percent of the decision to hire is based on the applicant's appearance. Dr. Albert Mehrabian's study on communication and attitude has shown that 55 percent of our believability and the way we are perceived is based on our body language, which includes posture, gestures, and eye contact. When people see you adjusting your clothes, picking at imaginary lint, jingling your keys, and scratching yourself, they become distracted. They lose confidence in you and in your message.

Here are just a few of the most common reasons why you may receive only a thundering silence from prospective employers and internal promotion interviewers after your interview has been completed:

1. Poor personality and manner; lack of poise; poor presentation of self; lack of self-confidence; timid; hesitant approach; arrogance, conceit.

2. Lack of goals and ambitions; does not show interest; uncertain, indecisive about the job or promotion in question.

3. Lack of enthusiasm and interest; no evidence of initiative.

4. Poor personal appearance and careless dress.

5. Unrealistic salary demands—more interested in salary than opportunity; unrealistic about promotion to top jobs.

6. Poor scholastic record without reasonable explanation for low grades.

7. Inability to express self well; poor speech habits and poor grammar.

8. Lack of maturity; no leadership potential.

9. Lack of preparation for the interview; failure to get information about the company and therefore unable to ask intelligent questions.

10. Lack of interest in the company and the type of job being offered.

11. Lack of extracurricular activities without good reason.

12. Attitude of "What can you do for me?"

13. Objection to travel; unwilling to relocate to branch offices or plants.

14. Immediate or prolonged military obligation.

15. No vocation jobs or other work experience; did not help finance own education.

Enhancing your image

Researchers have found people are attracted to others based on their appearance. When someone is dressed similarly to us, we infer they have similar beliefs, values, attitudes, and even political affiliation—so we are attracted to them. Our objective in meeting others is to establish comfort, trust, and rapport, which is not always easy. Physically attractive people are generally perceived as more likable, credible, and intelligent. Studies have shown that even juries are swayed by a person's appearance. Defendants who are considered more attractive and confident receive lighter sentences. Fair or not, it's a fact of life.

Let's take a look at what you can do to enhance your image. The best way to begin is to start in the morning in the bathroom. The moment you step into the shower, start thinking about the people you are meeting with today. What type of client will you be seeing? Are they conservative? Is their corporate dress fairly casual or more professional and conservative? Is this your first meeting or have you met with them before? When you come out of the shower, go to your closet and choose the clothes that will fit in with the style of those specific clients and in your scheduled meetings. During your drive to the office, it will be too late to change what you're wearing, so plan ahead.

You can build your executive wardrobe with key pieces (you probably already have) in your closet. You don't need to spend a small fortune to achieve a polished look. A personal shopper certainly isn't a requirement, but they are available to guide you toward some wise wardrobe choices. (Most retail stores do not charge for this service as they are paid a commission on your purchases.)

Dressing for success

Think about *how* you want to be perceived. What message do you want to communicate to your boss, your colleagues, and your clients? You have the opportunity to dress so the impressions formed by others will be the impressions *you want* them to form. (Your clothing is the first thing people notice about you—then your eyes, face, and gestures.) Here are some influential and positive ways to dress for success:

- Dress for the job you want, not the job you have. Notice how other people dress in the position you would like to have and dress in a similar way. In most situations, I believe you are better off being overdressed than underdressed. Would you prefer to go to a last-minute lunch with your boss dressed in blue jeans and a T-shirt or in dress pants and a tailored shirt or blouse?

- Build your wardrobe around neutral colors. Stick with "power" colors such as navy, black, gray, and camel. Accent your wardrobe with splashes of color and prints in shirts, ties, blouses, jackets, pants, skirts, and accessories. For example, a woman's navy blue suit looks great with a red blouse; a man's ordinary pinstripe suit makes a stronger statement when a burgundy or mauve tie is added.

- Invest in classics. Simplicity lasts for years. Stay away from fads and trends, which can be costly. No one is saying you should contribute to our national deficit, or to yours. You should, however, consider your priorities when it comes to your clothing budget. Think elegant, conservative, professional.

- Buy the best. Consider quality and fit. Most expensive does not mean better quality. Neither does a designer label. Check the stitching, seams, and hems for inferior work.

- Dress to suit specific occasions. When presenting to your company's board of directors, wear your most professional looking suit. Visiting a factory in 90-degree heat allows you to dress more casually and comfortably.

On the job

When meeting with a new client at his or her facility, or when interviewing at a company you have never visited, do your homework regarding dress code. Make a few telephone calls or stop by ahead of time to investigate. Call and request the company's annual report, study it, (you'll be able to ask intelligent questions about the company during your meeting), and observe the business attire worn by officers of the corporation and/or employees throughout the report. Clothing and accessories tell us a lot about a person. Dress well and you signal success, power, positive habits, and high status.

Studies have also linked clothing consciousness to higher salaries and positions held based on appearance. In their book, *The New Professional Image*, Susan Bixler and Nancy Nix-Rice discuss a study funded by Clairol Corporation and found it pays to dress for success. Judith Waters, Ph.D., a professor at Farleigh Dickinson University, sent out "before" photographs (improper, unprofessional image) and "after" photographs (*buffed and polished*, professional image) with identical resumes to over a thousand companies and asked them to determine a starting salary for each of the "candidates." (None of the companies received both "before" and "after" photos.) The results? Companies indicated an initial salary of 8 percent to 20 percent higher for those whose images had been upgraded in the "after" photos. For most positions, it's wise to forget about expressing your personal taste. Your clothes must convey the message you are competent, self-confident, reliable, and authoritative.

Color

Color plays an important role in our image. It helps us express ourselves as individuals, influences our impressions of others, and influences our emotions. Color reveals personality and can symbolize many things. It can be used, for example, to create positive environments in hospitals and office buildings. Fast-food restaurants use red, blue, and orange colors to create an accelerated, energetic atmosphere. The following is a list of some common psychological associations of colors.

- Red: Hot, dangerous, angry, passionate, sentimental, exciting, vibrant, and aggressive. It's the most physically provocative color and is perceived as a "power" color. If you are a shy person, incorporate red into your wardrobe in order to be viewed as assertive. A bold red tie on a man can be too blatant—wear a tie with flecks or stripes of red in it to add power. Wine, burgundy, rose, mauve, and dusty rose are other options.

- Orange: Lively, cheerful, joyous, warm, energetic, hopeful, and hospitable. Use this color conservatively. It can be too harsh and unbecoming to some skin tones. Brown-based earth tones somewhat related to orange are good middle-spectrum colors. These include terra-cotta, apricot, brick, or autumn-leaf tones.

- Yellow: Bright, sunny, cheerful, warm, prosperous, cowardly, and deceitful. It's most appropriate for casual clothing. Yellow is a bright color that attracts attention to itself and when it reflects onto the face, it can give the skin a sallow, jaundiced, unhealthy tinge. You would **not** want to wear this color on television.

- Green: Calm, cool, fresh, friendly, pleasant, balanced, restful, lucky, envious, and immature. Green is not an acceptable suit color for men or women, but teal or forest green can be incorporated in ties or sport coats for men and in suits, jackets, skirts, and scarves for women. There are numerous shades of green. Choose the one that works well with the basic pieces in your wardrobe.

- Blue: Peaceful, calm, restful, highly esteemed, serene, tranquil, truthful, cool, formal, and spacious. Navy blue is an excellent color to use as a base in your wardrobe. It works well with red, off-white, white, and pastel colors. Navy gives the feeling of individual authority when worn in business.

- Purple: Royal, dignified, powerful, rich, dominating, dramatic, mysterious, wise, and passionate. Works well for a woman's blouse or for an accent color in a man's tie. Mauves, rich royal purple, dark violet, dusty violet, deep lilac shades, and plum purples are all flattering colors.

- White: Innocent, youthful, faithful, pure, and peaceful. Excellent accent color. Use white for shirts and blouses and winter white for blazers, slacks, trousers, and skirts. Be aware that white makes everything appear larger and can add pounds to your image when in front of a camera. (The camera **does** add ten pounds.) Winter white works well with black and navy. For women, pearls are always an excellent accessory with winter white. When *dressing up,* my favorite color is a winter white monochromatic look with a strand of pearls—looks great at a wedding *or* dining out.

- Black: Mysterious, tragic, serious, sad, signified, silent, old, sophisticated, strong, and wise. Can be a "downer" color, due to its association with funerals, but is the best choice for formal attire. Black is another strong "power" color, so use it carefully. It can appear harsh against most skin tones, however, it's still the best daytime color for women who appear frequently in public. Black is a *slimming* color. Most of my basics are black or navy blue; psychologically, I always feel "thinnest" in those colors.

- Gray: Modest, sad, and old. Works well with black, white, and navy. Banker's gray denotes confidence, trustworthiness, success, and authority. Some shades of gray may look better with your skin tone than others. Hold the gray item up to your face in front of a mirror and make sure it's not washing the color from your face. Gray can be an excellent choice for the public person because it does not attract attention to itself. It's a quiet color and can be worn in any setting, making a strong statement of strength while at the same time making you appear approachable.

Certain colors will look better with your skin tone than others will. It's important to wear the colors that make you feel good and which cause you to receive the most compliments. There are categories each person falls into with his or her skin tone, hair color, eyes, and so forth. If you haven't had your "colors" done (men **and** women), I strongly recommend you find out which shades and tones work best for you. Build your basics around these colors and you're on your way to looking more professional and polished. In short, your clothes should work for you, not overpower you. Learn to play up your assets and camouflage your liabilities.

Accessorizing

Most cakes need frosting, and most wardrobes need accessorizing. Accessories play an important role in our appearance and in how we are perceived. A component of your credibility can be expressed through the use of unique, eye-catching accessories such as a brightly colored scarf or tie, an unstructured suit, a bold neck piece, a belt, or bold-patterned fabric. Visualize the professional you want to be and project something unique but appropriate for your profession.

Accessories for men

For men, the following are a few examples of ways to easily enhance your look.

- Belts: High quality leather belt in black, brown, or cordovan, about one-inch wide with a subtle metal buckle, makes a suit look more expensive. Crocodile and alligator look great, but I recommend staying away from the *real thing*. Your boss, a person in your office, or a potential client could be offended by your choice.

- Braces: Not the clip-on variety but in silk, with leather attachments. Don't wear a belt. Your tie should reach the **top** of your waistband. Pants worn with braces should be at least one-half inch larger in the waistline. They should coordinate with, but not match, the necktie. The attachments should be leather and button inside the trouser.

- Handkerchief: Cotton, linen, or silk are the best fabric choices. This accessory is an excellent way to upgrade a business suit. Patterned silk needn't match the tie but should complement it. Stick with small patterns or solid colors. Beware of retailers who sell matching ties and pocket squares; this duo will brand you as unfashionable. Use a clean handkerchief every day—several if you are dealing with a cold or have allergies.

- **Always wear a long-sleeved shirt with your suit** and make sure it appears to have been professionally pressed. The tip of your necktie should reach the **top** of your belt buckle. When in doubt about what color shirt to wear, choose white. White is classic, traditional, and always correct.

- Small cuff links: The most updated looks are gold or silver bars or balls, matte stones such as onyx lapis, and rectangular or square shapes. Think elegant, conservative, and subtle. Tie bars and tie tacks are out of fashion.

- An elegant watch: 14K gold is well worth the investment. Leather bands are certainly an option to consider. Avoid metal, bendable watch bands, heavy sport watches, cartoon characters, and novelty designs.

- Keep jewelry to a minimum. Men should **never** wear gold chains around their neck. Necklaces and business are like oil and water—they don't mix. Maximum, one ring per hand. When in doubt, leave your college ring in your jewelry box.

- Ties: The smaller the knot, the more formal and affluent the message. Silk ties make the best knots. As for matching lapel, collar, and tie widths, with rare exceptions, like follows like—skinny lapel, skinny collar, thin tie.

- Socks: A pattern or print adds interest to your wardrobe, but don't get too carried away. Make sure they are able to stay up around mid-calf of the leg. A bare, hairy leg is not a pretty sight and quickly takes away from your credibility. I once worked with a client who, when uncomfortable or nervous, would pull his pant leg up past his calf to the point where his bare leg and sock would show. This was a habit he didn't realize he had, and it did nothing to enhance his credibility. Check the status of your socks when seated. (Have you ever noticed men on talks shows and how distracting it is to see their bare, hairy leg exposed? Keep yours covered, please!)

- Thinner-soled shoes: More elegant and tasteful. The thinner the sole (no more than one-quarter-inch thick), the more expensive the shoes appear. Resole shoes with badly worn heels. Tassel loafers are acceptable with business suits in some corporate cultures; wing-tips portray a more conservative look. Stay away from thick-soled shoes—you don't want to look like you just got off the turnip truck.

- Fabrics: Wool blends de-wrinkle quickly with wool crepe being the best choice as well as the most comfortable. Cotton weighs nothing, so it's nice for summer travel. Corduroy makes your butt look bigger. Polyester, born again as *microfiber* but with the Sybilline capacity to adopt personalities as varied as viscose and ramie, is now pliable and an acceptable option. When looking for low-maintenance, low-cost clothes that travel well, stay away from linen.

Accessories for women

Women can add distinction to their wardrobe with accessories, but they should not become the main attraction. A few genuine pieces, worn discreetly, are always in the best of taste. A modest outfit can triple its face value when worn with an excellent quality handbag, shoes, and jewelry. In addition to their style-enhancing abilities, accessories are often long-term investments. For example, a quality silk scarf can last for decades and immediately enhance the look of an outfit. Anything that sparkles, shines, dangles, rattles, or makes noise distracts and takes away from your professional image and what you are saying. The following are a few examples of ways a woman can enhance her image.

- Lapel pins: Bold when wearing few accessories. Signature pins and pins with interesting designs would be good additions to your accessory collection.

- Simple gold watch, thin band—14K gold is the best investment. If the watch you want isn't within your price range, find a watch similar to the watch you would like to buy. Avoid clunky watches and cartoon characters on the face of the watch—you want to be taken seriously in the workplace.

- Classic leather belts; designer buckles optional. A great belt immediately dresses up a pair of slacks or a skirt while adding polish to your overall look. The belt should match the slacks or skirt for the most elongated, slimming look.

- Shoes: Stick with closed-toe leather pumps that have heels one to three inches in height. They are slenderizing and professional. High stiletto heels are out and negatively affect a woman's credibility; strappy sandals show too much foot and also inhibit the stride. Spend as much as you can afford on a few pairs of plain, good looking, comfortable leather shoes and keep them in perfect condition. Shoe color should match your hemline, hosiery, or appear darker, which also lengthens your look. Regarding tennis shoes: Even the most upscale sneakers are **never** appropriate for business wear. When walking to the office, change into a dressier shoe the moment you arrive.

- To make your legs appear thinner, wear monochromatic hosiery. With a black skirt, wear black hose; with a navy skirt, wear navy hose. Choose shoes in the same dark color. Your legs appear longer, thus lengthening your overall look. Neutral-colored hosiery is the strongest look for business. Bright colors are inappropriate. For the most slimming look, match your jacket with the skirt and/or slacks. You must always wear hosiery, no matter how tan your legs may be or how hot and muggy the weather.

- Gold earrings, no larger than a nickel and preferably 14K gold or sterling silver. Invest in one good pair with screw-on backs or French clips so you won't lose them. Eliminate gaudy, costume jewelry from your wardrobe. Long, dangling earrings are distracting and unprofessional.

- Pearls: Always a classic choice and it's not necessary to buy the most expensive. Some stores have such good quality, you can get by without spending a small fortune but look as if you did. An 18- to 20-inch single strand of pearls is the most versatile length with a plain sweater and dressy pair of slacks offers a clean, crisp, elegant look. Add a pair of pearl earrings and you'll look terrific!

- Daytime diamonds: Less is more. Try not to be too flashy with your diamonds. Some female clients wear a wedding ring while on business trips even though they're not married—an excellent way to keep unwanted advances at bay.

- A note regarding nails and nail polish: Nails should be one-eighth to one-quarter inch beyond the tip of the fingers. Buff or polish the nail. If you choose to wear polish, stick with lightly tinted or softer shades. I prefer a neutral polish, especially for an important meeting, when presenting, or speaking to groups—

I don't want my nail polish to become the focus of my gestures. Lighter colors are also easier to maintain; darker colors require more frequent touchups.

Accessories for men and women

Many accessories pertain to both men and women.

- Eyeglasses: Eye contact is of utmost importance—tinted lenses are taboo. Choose functional frames with clear, nonglare lenses. Tortoise frames or thin, wire frames create an intense, intelligent look. Studies have shown that people who wear glasses are perceived as more intelligent and more successful. For younger clients needing to appear older, I suggest eyeglasses with clear, nonglare lenses—even if you don't *need* to wear eyeglasses to see. They can also be used as an accessory when presenting: Wear them *through* your introduction, which should be delivered to your audience without having to look at your notes, remove them, and put them back on before the conclusion of your presentation. Practice this gesture or you will appear phony and insincere. (For a man, the glasses can be put into the breast pocket of his jacket; for a woman, the glasses can be placed on a table or into her jacket pocket.) **Never** "suck" on the bow of your eyeglasses, even if you are "thinking" about what you're going to say next or pondering a question.

- High-quality fountain pens, antique pens, and designer label pens create prestige. Invest in one good pen—Mont Blanc or Waterman is a good choice. Carry it with you everywhere and *remember* to use it. **Do not** ask a client to sign a ten-thousand-dollar order with a ninety-nine-cent pen. Carry a fine pen and pencil set, as befits someone who writes important documents. Make sure you keep pens, pencils, and order forms handy. Don't ruin the magic moment of closing a sale by fumbling for the tools of your trade. High quality writing instruments contribute to a polished, professional image.

- An expensive-looking leather briefcase is another excellent accessory. Soft-sided and satchel types are the most current style.

Take care of it and it will last for years. Coach makes one of the best briefcases on the market for both men and women. I've had the same black soft-sided briefcase for more than ten years. Applying leather lotion to it on a regular basis has truly extended its life. It still looks like new. Another option to consider is a top-quality leather portfolio that creates a sleek, clean look.

- Your business card is part of your personal and corporate image. It should always be printed on excellent card stock and should not be folded, torn, or dirty. **Never** give anyone a card with a crossed-out telephone number or address. This is part of your first impression. Always carry a supply in your day-planner or briefcase. It amazes me when I meet with a client and they don't have a business card with them. I recently met a woman at a seminar. When I asked for her business card so we could exchange information, she "didn't have one with her." How these people succeed in business is beyond me! When between jobs, have a quality card printed with your home address and telephone number on it. More than thirty million business cards are exchanged every day; it's the most common and inexpensive way to promote yourself.

- One of the strongest, personal business assets we have is our teeth. Brush at least twice a day. If you don't floss already, start now. Flossing will eliminate 90 percent of mouth odor because decayed food is removed more efficiently. When lunching with a client or if you have a business meeting scheduled for later in the day, avoid garlic, onions, salsa, Italian sausage, and so forth. Keep an extra toothbrush and toothpaste in your desk to use after lunch or before the meeting. Nothing spoils the impact of your image quicker than having spinach or pepper stuck between your teeth during a business lunch. Proper care and regular visits to the dentist can work wonders. There are many ways to enhance your smile. Whether you need to cap, bond, bleach, crown, or straighten your teeth, investing in them is one of the best ways to increase your chances of making a great first impression. Your teeth are part of the immediate first impression you make on others.

The impression you make on others does not begin and end at the office. It carries over into the evening and weekend. You never know when you might run into a client or colleague at the grocery store, dry cleaners, or video store. Always look polished and pulled together. **Never** leave your house without giving yourself a *once-over* to make sure you won't be embarrassed if you run into someone you aren't expecting to see. Have you ever run into an "old flame" or someone you went to school with and wished you had spent more time on your appearance? It never fails...when you least expect it, that's when you will trip over the last person you want to see.

When traveling, wear a suit or executive casual coordinates on the plane. You'll receive better service from airline personnel and your seating companion may turn out to be a valuable new business connection. (I've acquired quite a few new clients just by having a pleasant conversation with the person seated next to me and being an excellent listener.)

Your mirror image

Give yourself a thirty-second "pep talk" in the mirror every morning. Tell yourself how wonderful you are, how terrific you look, how smart you are, what a great asset you are to the company, and how lucky they are to have you. (I realize this may sound silly, but it works!) The good feelings generated by "your talk" will create an aura of confidence, energy, and enthusiasm. You will positively affect everyone you come into contact with throughout the day. If you become upset about something during the day, don't carry it around like baggage. Get over it and get on with other important matters. Tell yourself (more) positive affirmations at night, before going to sleep—you'll wake up feeling refreshed and excited about the day.

The common denominator to all of the successful people I have worked with is this: They are excellent communicators. They know how to talk to people and in the process of a conversation, get what they want. Here are a few examples of what it takes to be successful:

- **Confidence.** You are not afraid to ask for what you want.

- **Appreciation.** You show your appreciation of people when you **do get** what you want.

- **Consistency.** You are constantly nurturing relationships and maintaining open lines of communication, not only when you **want** something from a person, but on a regular basis.

- **Persistence.** You never give up. No matter what the situation, you try another strategy or find a way to achieve your goals and objectives.

- **Attention to others.** You are an excellent listener. You keep an open mind and listen to both negative and positive opinions; most people talk too much and should learn to listen more.

- **Resilience.** You bounce back quickly from rejection or depression. You know that your feelings show through your emotions, tone of voice, and attitude so you never allow yourself time for "pity parties."

- **Friendliness and approachability.** You always offer a greeting to anyone you meet or come into contact with. You offer praise and recognition on a regular basis and never wait until an important meeting to make an announcement about a job well done.

By working to develop and enhance these areas of your life, your relationships with your boss, colleagues, clients, family, and friends will improve dramatically. Along the way, you will also realize an increased amount of self-confidence and self-esteem.

The impact of your business casual wardrobe

Business casual has become more prevalent in the workplace. Casual dressing allows for greater flexibility in wardrobe choices, but for many, it adds to an already growing sense of confusion and insecurity about what to wear. Whatever your personal level of enthusiasm for casual dressing, understanding it is a must in today's business climate. Your visual image communicates its message constantly, whether you are wearing denim, Dockers, or a double-breasted blazer. The wider range of looks and the related messages sent when in business casual can create too many opportunities for error to leave the matter to chance. There is no single, clear-cut casual look for all situations for men or women. Some executives forego casual day dressing if they have an important meeting or client lunch. As one executive puts it, "My company doesn't dictate how I dress...my customers do."

On the office grapevine, clothes speak louder than words. Do you know what messages you are sending? The first rule is: No matter what you wear, you should feel comfortable. The physical comfort of your clothes is the underpinning for your emotional comfort. Emotional comfort is largely a matter of familiarity. If you decide to change your image, do it slowly, so you don't appear uncomfortable with your *new look.*

At a company where the dress code is extremely informal (such as a factory), pressed jeans, Dockers, cotton twill, or corduroy slacks with a collared knit or cotton shirt are acceptable for men and women. I generally recommend staying away from blue jeans and sweatshirts, no matter what the situation. White, tan, or black jeans can be dressed up more easily than a pair of blue jeans. If "everyone wears jeans, including my boss," opt for a clean, crisp, informal look. Press and/or starch your jeans (**never** roll up the cuffs), wear a belt if you tuck your shirt or blouse in, and polish your loafers.

When wearing sneakers, make sure they are washed and in good shape. No sweat pants or jogging suits; you don't want to look like a complete slob just because you can dress more informally. On days when you are cleaning out office files, participating in a weekend retreat, going to a ball game, or playing football at the company picnic, the above options are considerations when deciding what to wear.

At a company where the dress code is informal yet not quite as relaxed (such as in a small office), men should wear a pair of well-pressed slacks with a matching sports shirt and well-maintained footwear like penny or tassel loafers. A good quality cotton sweater, an unstructured sportcoat, or a corduroy jacket are other options. Women should wear denim, cotton or corduroy skirts/pants with a knit shirt, cotton blouse, cardigan sweater, or belted, casual jacket. No leggings or spandex pants. Casual shoes include tassel loafers, espadrilles, and leather flats. Keep accessories to a minimum.

At a company where the dress code is casual but more formal (such as in a larger corporation), men should wear well-pressed khakis, chinos, or trousers with a colored or subtly patterned shirt. A casual jacket or blazer can be worn with polo-style shirts that are well-pressed and crisp. Additional choices include pullover sweaters, contrasting vests, or cardigans. Polished leather loafers and minimal coordinated accessories will pull together a professional image. Women should wear wool, wool-blend, or linen-like gabardine pants or classic tailored trousers with coordinating blouses, tops, sweaters, vests, jackets, and blazers—no tank tops or camisoles. Stick with basic colors—nothing wild or flashy. Flat leather shoes or tailored, woven loafers and casual, minimal accessories are excellent choices for a clean, tailored look.

"Executive casual" is the best choice for managers and executives, especially in high-profile, large corporations. Tailored separates work well for important internal meetings and presentations. For men, a high-quality lightweight wool or wool-blend trouser with a long-sleeved, well-pressed shirt or fine-gauge cotton, silk, or cashmere sweater looks great. A coordinated sportcoat or blazer (casual tie optional), along with a gold watch and gold ring present a commanding visual presence. Women should wear a matching or coordinated pantsuit or skirted suit in silk, wool crepe, gabardine, or knit. (St. John or Helen Sui knits are excellent choices for travel.) A long-sleeved silk or high-quality cotton blouse, silk, or cashmere sweater, topped off with a silk scarf looks sensational. Conservative accessories are a must; pearls provide a dash of elegance. Add a low-heeled leather pump, black patent pump, or dressy flats and you will look like you are ready to run the company!

Men and women

- Make sure your shoes are polished and in excellent condition. Nothing robs you of your polished image faster than a pair of tacky-looking shoes.

- Build a small assortment of top-quality casual garments. Investment buys add up over the years and are the foundation of a successful, classy, casual wardrobe.

- The choices you make as you create your own image, whether it's strictly business or business casual, can transmit a positive statement about you and about what you think about yourself.

- Whether you are a business executive, lobbyist, salesperson, or domestic god or goddess, *you* set the tone for the entire day by your morning rituals and the wardrobe choices you make.

Once you are confident your clothes work for *you* and fit *your* image, you can forget all about them and know that no matter what the situation, you are ready to face your colleagues, clients, reporters, or a national television audience.

CHAPTER 2

The Handshake

There are additional ways you can make your first impression a memorable one. One way is with a crisp, firm, warm handshake. A limp and effortless handshake usually matches a person's personality. Clasp palm to palm (not palm to fingers), web to web, look the person in the eye, and **smile!** Try to match the other person's grip—not outdo him or her. Be firm but not so forceful you cause discomfort. One or two good pumps is all that's needed. Whether you are male or female, initiate the handshake. Gender is no longer a consideration. (Children should begin shaking hands by the age of four.)

Handshaking customs vary from country to country. The French shake hands when entering and leaving a room. The Germans pump hands one time only. Some Africans snap their fingers after each handshake to signify freedom; others consider handshaking in bad taste. Whatever the situation, find out the local custom before assuming your brand of handshake will be acceptable. The firmness of the typical male handshake in the United States probably originated in contests of strength, such as Indian wrestling.

In the United States, shake hands when saying "hello" and "good-bye." When you run into someone outside the office, shake hands. A good handshake is essential to making the best impression. A person who offers their hand for the handshake is perceived as more self-confident and assured. **Always** begin an important meeting with a handshake and a smile. Human nature being what it is, if we send out a positive message with a friendly handshake, we will more likely get a positive message in return. If we send out a negative message, we will get negative feedback. Communication is a two-way street between you and the person you are meeting and begins with a first impression that includes your greeting.

If you are seated when being introduced, stand up and shake the person's hand. This communicates you are pleased to meet the person. By staying seated, you convey a message of disinterest and rudeness. A lot can be learned about a person by their handshake. A hearty handshake implies you are personable, positive, and glad to meet the other person. A lifeless, fishy handshake suggests an insecure, lifeless person. **Never** take someone's fingers as part of your handshake. A person who offers their fingers as their handshake is perceived as uncertain and lacking confidence.

Along with the handshake, sweaty palms can be a concern. An excellent way to combat this is to spray an antiperspirant on your hands the night before your important meeting, at bedtime. Shower in the morning and you'll be cool as a cucumber when it comes time to shake hands. Another option is to carry a handkerchief with you and discreetly wipe your hands before meeting someone, then offer your hand. At a cocktail party, hold your drink in your *left* hand so your right hand is free for the handshake.

When attending conferences, trade shows, conventions, and other meetings, you are often given a badge or name tag. The tendency is to place it on the left side. Because many of us are right-handed, it's easier to pin it on that way and it looks better in the mirror. However, that's not what etiquette expert Letticia Baldridge suggests. She says the name tag belongs on the *right-hand* side of the chest. When a person shakes hands, the eye naturally follows the line of the arm and focuses first on the other person's right shoulder, then on the properly placed name tag, making it quick and easy to read.

Introductions

We are usually hearing a person's name for the first time during an introductory handshake. Distracted by our own discomfort, we may not be paying enough attention to actually hear their name. Relax; memory improves when you are at ease. To help remember a person's name, immediately repeat his or her name aloud in the first sentence you use during your reply. If possible and appropriate, try to use it again within the next two or three minutes. People like to hear their name spoken. You don't want to use it so often that it becomes tedious and sounds insincere—they may think you have a name disorder. By using it (occasionally) during your conversation, it will help you remember the individual's name and, at the same time, make a positive impact.

Far more rude than forgetting a name is not introducing people at all. People are uncomfortable when they're not introduced as part of the group. A common mistake people make is avoiding the introduction of someone they know because they have forgotten his or her name. Don't let a memory lapse stop you from using your manners properly. There are ways you can get around this. One way is to admit you're human: "I apologize, I've forgotten your name" or "I have it on the tip of my tongue, but just can't seem to remember." One apology is enough. The person will usually understand and help you out.

When there are people to introduce at a business meeting, remember that gender, age, and even rank are secondary. If you are introducing your boss to a customer, the **customer is always mentioned first** because they are the most important. For example, Mr. Jones is the President of ABC Company and is one of your customers. He would be introduced **to** your manager, John Doe. "Mr. Jones, I would like you to meet my manager, John Doe. John, this is Mr. Jones, the President of ABC Company."

When two people of equal rank are introduced, the woman is introduced first or honor the person from outside your organization first. Introduce an older person to a younger person. Introduce a person you know more to a person you know less. Introduce a peer in your company to a peer in another company. Don't make wisecracks or try to be funny at another person's expense. Mention something the two people have in common to stimulate interaction such as hobbies, travels, children, or pets. **Say first the name of the person to whom you want to show greatest respect or honor.**

When a man and woman are introduced and he is the president of the firm and she is the administrative assistant of the same firm, the president is introduced first. For example: "Mr. Smith, I would like you to meet Jane Doe; Jane does an excellent job in our public affairs office." Honor and give added recognition to the person who is first mentioned and introductions will be easy and correct.

At dinner parties or political gatherings, always present the older person, guest of honor, or dignitary first. Be sure to use titles, not first names, when introducing a much older person, a doctor (physician, psychologist, or veterinarian), a member of the clergy, or someone of official rank. Use the dignitary's title even if he or she is retired or no longer holds that position. When introducing a widow, give both her given and her late husband's names.

An obvious breach of etiquette is calling someone by a name *you* prefer, not the name *they* prefer. An unflattering or juvenile name has no place in business. If Charles prefers to be called Charles, that is what you should call him and how you should introduce him—not as Chuck or Charlie.

When attending a seminar, convention, or company party and you see someone you want to meet but no one has introduced you to the person, why not introduce yourself? Take the initiative, smile, shake hands, and introduce yourself. Be direct, honest, genuine, and personable. Establish rapport by complimenting the other person, volunteer information about yourself, or identify common interests, hobbies, and acquaintances. Avoid off-color remarks and stay away from touchy subjects. It's safer to joke about the weather than to say something inappropriate about religion or politics. Do not monopolize the conversation. Ask questions, listen attentively, and *appear* interested, even if the person has a tendency to go on and on. Be open and honest during this conversation; you may wind up with a new friend or future client.

Some people are confused about using a person's first name in an introduction or during conversation. If you have to think about whether or not you should use a first name, then don't. Use both first and last names when introducing and you won't have to worry about what is appropriate. Even if a person says, "Call me John," you will start off on a better foot if you respect the person and properly introduce him or her.

There are some circumstances where introductions are not appropriate. One example would be when you know two people do not want to be introduced. "Jane" may be a member of PETA, an organization against wearing fur, and the other person may be wearing a fur coat. Introducing them may cause an unpleasant disturbance. Another example is if you are in a public place and it's too noisy for introductions. If you can find a quiet area, fine. Otherwise it's not necessary to try to shout above the crowd.

When you are expecting several people and they arrive separately, introduce each person as he or she arrives. During our seminars, as each participant arrives, the group is politely interrupted and introduced to the newcomer. They are left to mingle, and as each new person arrives, he or she is introduced to the group. Once all participants have been introduced, they are given approximately five minutes to get acquainted before we begin. (If someone is late, which is rude, we begin without him or her.) Once he or she does arrive, the person is given a minute to collect themselves, *then* brought into the training room and introduced to everyone.

Just remember: The main rule of good manners in greeting people and making introductions is consideration for everyone. Even if you don't know the precise etiquette, by putting people at ease and showing proper respect, your actions will be acceptable.

CHAPTER 3

The Power of Professional Presence

Improving your posture, balance, stance

Posture, balance, and stance are additional areas of crucial influence relating to first impressions. Appropriate attire and a firm handshake are not enough. Posture tells us how a person feels about him- or herself and how comfortable he or she is with a particular setting—it can provide important clues about personality and character. There are three main kinds of posture: standing, sitting, and lying down.

When standing in front of a group or when speaking one-to-one, you want to appear strong, in control, and self-confident. Good posture does this for you. It enhances your voice quality, makes you appear more successful, and makes you look taller. (Statistics have shown that taller people make more money than shorter people.) Poor posture makes you appear weak, mild, and meek. A slumped body with rounded back, bowed head, and sloping shoulders makes you appear shorter and sends out signals of vulnerability, insecurity, disinterest, and low self-esteem.

Maintain a relaxed, energetic posture with eyes and head level, shoulders back, chin up, and stomach in. Yes, you need to tuck in your tummy—a strong posture can take ten pounds off the way you look! Distribute your weight evenly: Place your feet shoulder width apart with knees slightly bent and relaxed. Head, shoulders, and chest are directly over one another. Do not rock, sway, or shift—think "cement."

Resting one leg while putting more weight on the other, a *low balance,* takes away from your overall image and credibility. You probably don't even realize you do this because it's a *comfortable habit.* This stance negatively affects your shoulder line, which should be erect, yet relaxed. Your off-center posture may cause others to perceive you as having an attitude or appearing disinterested and bored with the conversation. Do not cross your legs when standing—it makes you appear nervous, shy, and insecure. Shifting your weight from foot to foot is distracting as well. Again, keep your weight evenly distributed, feet shoulder width apart. You will be standing on solid ground and appear more relaxed, centered, and focused.

Watch the posture of people at office gatherings or meetings. Those outside the action hold different postures from those involved with what is going on. Outsiders stand with their weight on one foot rather than on both. Someone more closely involved stands with the weight evenly distributed on both feet, leaning forward, and with the head held forward. Leaning away from a situation signals disinterest, noninvolvement, distaste. Note: The higher the status of the person you are talking to, the more inclined you are to face him or her.

Be aware of constant nodding or bobbing of your head, making you appear overly anxious or eager to please. A cocked or tilted head can suggest confusion and simple-mindedness **or** can be perceived as flirtatious, seductive, and vulnerable. What's happening with your head movement during casual conversation or when presenting information? Too much nodding takes away your influence. You don't want to look like the dog in the back window of a '57 Chevy with the head bobbing and nodding. If anything, you will appear too eager to please and overly anxious. Keep your head level and your chin up.

What should I do with my hands?

It's interesting to realize what happens with our hands when we are experiencing any amount of tension: Clenching fists, twiddling thumbs, moving fingers (like lobster claws), or playing with jewelry is distracting. Some people pop the top of a magic marker on and off with one hand. Others extend and retract a collapsible pointer without being aware of how annoying it is to everyone else in the room. Absentmindedly clicking your pen, tapping your fingers, stroking your beard, scratching your nose, licking your lips, adjusting your glasses, or playing with your hair are all distractions and mannerisms that may be *comfortable habits* you need to eliminate.

You want to come across as confident yet approachable, relaxed but not sloppy, and credible but not stiff. To do this, assume what is called the *neutral* position: Hang your arms loosely at your sides so they are free to gesture and in sync with the message you are attempting to deliver. I guarantee this will feel uncomfortable, stiff, and even rigid at first, but this simple, *neutral* posture is incredibly powerful. (It takes practice.) When you master this posture, you will be perceived as self-confident, believable, credible, and authoritative.

Keep your hands out of your pockets. If you do put your hands into your pockets, remove your keys and change. No jingling allowed! This is another annoying habit many people have and can be as irritating as fingernails on a blackboard. As discussed in *How to Read a Person Like a Book* by Gerald I. Nierenberg and Henry H. Calero, Dr. Sandor Feldman observed "people who constantly jingle money in their pockets are very much concerned with money or lack of it." (Louis B. Mayer used to jingle coins constantly in his pants pocket. When asked why he did it, he replied, "To remind me of the time I didn't have any.") **Force yourself** to allow your arms to hang loosely at your sides. Hold your head up and talk. It takes supreme discipline to just stand there, but you can do it! (One hand in a pocket while the other is free to gesture is acceptable.)

Another benefit of relaxing your arms at your sides is that you will have more freedom to gesture, which we discuss in greater detail during Chapter 5. Stay away from the "fig leaf" position (remember Adam and Eve?), which is a protective stance. It's difficult to *let go* once the hands have been clasped in front of or behind the body. With hands clasped in front of the body, you may be wringing them or twiddling your thumbs and not even be aware of what you are doing—hardly fitting for someone making a forceful presentation.

Placing your hands on your hips with legs in an open stance can make you appear aggressive and/or authoritative. Psychologically, you may want to appear larger. Stand upright rather than leaning against a door, a wall or furniture. Slumping or leaning makes you look lazy and does not add to your credibility. Hands on the hips has been identified as a "readiness" posture. You often see it during a sports event when an athlete is waiting to become involved. Depending upon the person and the situation, the perception of the subtext can differ.

Crossing the arms and legs

Whether standing or sitting, a *comfortable habit* for many is to cross the arms. When both arms are folded across the chest, your influence and image are diminished. Although you may be cold and your arms are crossed as a means of insulation, you could be perceived as protecting yourself or hiding from an unfavorable situation. In a face-to-face setting, crossed arms usually signal disagreement, negativity, or a closed mind. A partial arm barrier, such as holding onto one arm at the elbow, generally signals that a person lacks self-confidence or is a stranger to the group. Dr. Albert Mehrabian made an interesting study about posture and a woman's use of space. When sitting, she will adopt an open-arm, relaxed posture in the presence of someone she likes. When the arms are folded across her chest, it indicates defensiveness, indifference, or dislike.

Crossing the legs when seated can have a devastating effect on a negotiation. In a study described in *How to Read a Person Like a Book*, Gerald L. Nierenberg and Henry H. Calero found after videotaping two thousand transactions, no sales were made by people who had their legs crossed. If you want your prospect to receive your message as being cooperative and trustworthy, you are better off if you do not cross your legs. With your legs uncrossed, your feet flat on the floor, and your body tilted toward your prospect, you have a better chance of sending your prospect an open, positive signal.

Nierenberg and Calero also observed other stages of negotiations when issues were presented and discussed or when heated arguments took place, and one or both of the negotiators had their legs crossed. The number of negotiations where settlements were reached increased tremendously when both negotiators uncrossed their legs and moved toward each other. In other recordings of such confrontations, **no** settlements were ever reached when one of the negotiators *still* had crossed legs. Individuals who cross his or her legs seem to be the ones who give you the most competition or need the greatest amount of attention.

Crossing both the arms and legs while seated means the person has most likely withdrawn from the conversation. **Crossing both the arms and legs while standing** is considered a *double-negative* and is a defensive or closed-standing posture. You are taking up less space, making you appear timid, unsure, and lacking in confidence. At your next cocktail party or company function, do some people-watching. How many are standing with their arms or legs crossed—or both? How do they look? Confident? Secure? Assertive? Or lacking in confidence, insecure, shy, and withdrawn? Practice strong posture during casual conversation, when meeting a colleague in the hallway, or while standing in line at the bank. You'll be surprised at how much concentration it initially takes. *Old, bad, comfortable habits* die a slow painful death. Stand (or sit) up straight, look people in the eye, and stop fidgeting!

Whether you are standing or sitting, walking through the corporate offices, receiving a tour of a manufacturing plant, or entering a cocktail party, good posture makes you appear as if you have more energy, stamina, and confidence than a person with a burdensome carriage.

Use of space

In the United States, we prefer 2 to 3 feet of space between our self and the person to whom we are speaking This is considered our personal "comfort zone" and is equal to about an arm's length. Move closer to the person. How does the person react when you invade his or her space? By backing away? Now, step back 2 feet. Does the person walk toward you to eliminate the distance? Don't stand too close or too far away—be comfortable.

When traveling to other countries, read about their culture so you are not offended by them and they are not offended by you. In Roger Axtell's book, *Gestures, The Do's and Taboos of Body Language Around the World*, he discusses how Asians usually stand *farther* apart. In contrast, Latinos and Middle Easterners stand *much closer*—sometimes even toe-to-toe or side-to-side brushing elbows. As a result, North Americans need to prepare themselves for such close encounters because to move away sends an unfriendly message.

We rarely think of space when we think of body language, but manipulation of space can be an important business tool. The subtext of power and status is seen during business meetings, lunches, interviews, and even while standing in an elevator. The positioning of your body, whether or not there is a desk or table between you and the other person, even the angle of the chairs when seated, plays an important role in how we use our personal space. A desk or table can serve as a protective device to keep a person at a distance in your office. This sends a subtext of formality without equality, creating a barrier between you and the other person.

To reduce formality and make a person feel more relaxed, eliminate the barriers by bringing a chair closer to the corner of your desk or sit on a chair *next to* the person. Another option is to sit next to a person on a couch, angling your body toward them. One arm along the back of the couch (the arm positioned at an angle), with your body inclined toward the other, sends a subtext of interest and involvement. Leaning back and away from a person signals disinterest or disbelief.

During a business lunch, each person prefers his or her *half* of the table. Psychologically, there is an invisible line down the middle of the table. Try this "experiment" the next time you go to lunch with a friend or colleague: Place the salt, pepper, ketchup, or bud vase on *your friend's side* of the table. What happens to his or her body language? You will see it makes the person uncomfortable because you are invading *his or her space*. Most self-confident individuals discreetly move the item(s) back into the middle of the table or off to the side. Others become quiet or begin to fidget. When both diners feel their space is appropriate, communication improves and becomes more relaxed.

The need for *our space* is all around us. Whether in our car, at lunch, or in an elevator, we want the distance between us and other people to be comfortable. The next time you're in an elevator, study what happens with each person's body language and his or her use of space. Notice how everyone readjusts their positions when a person gets on or off the elevator. We prefer our own personal *bubble of space* and don't like it when someone invades it. The same is true when driving our automobile. No one likes a tailgater.

Sitting

When invited to sit in a person's office, whether it's a meeting with your manager or your first meeting with a customer, always choose the arm chair over a couch or loveseat. The couch/loveseat forces you into a weaker posture. If it's at all cushy, you will sink into it. When you attempt to rise, you will appear clumsy as you try to pull yourself up from it. An arm chair provides you with a more rigid back creating stronger posture; it also allows you to be more expansive with your gestures.

When approaching a chair, pause to keep your upper and lower body in alignment. Maintain a strong posture, bend your knees, and deliberately lower your body onto the chair. Sit on the edge of the chair first. Using your thigh muscles, slowly push yourself into the back of the chair. When standing, reverse the sequence. While seated, rest one of your arms on the arm of the chair; rest your other arm, at an angle, across the back of the same chair. Stay away from folding your hands politely in your lap or fidgeting. If you are not comfortable *taking up space*, you can rest each of your arms on the arms of the chair. Either way, you appear more relaxed, confident, and authoritative.

In a meeting setting, whenever possible, sit at a table at an angle to the person with whom you are meeting. This provides a more relaxed atmosphere. As mentioned earlier, a desk creates a barrier. To make a person feel more comfortable, get out from behind your desk.

Once you have been seated in a conference room setting, if there is an empty chair next to you, physically get up and move it away from the table. Reposition your chair and take up more space. Sitting next to an empty chair takes away your influence—you want to appear as confident and authoritative as possible. Spread your notes and paperwork out on the table. Be expansive with your use of space. Keep your hands out of your lap and on the table. The best look we have found when videotaping a person (while seated) is to gently place one hand on top of the other. This posture allows you the freedom to naturally gesture while speaking. Don't fold hands in a clasped mode on the table as this limits your gestures.

When needing buy-in or approval from colleagues, sit next to them on their dominant side, even if you don't like them or you know they are not fond of you. If they are right-handed, sit to their right; if they are left-handed, sit to their left. Psychologically, this increases your chances of getting them to go along with your idea. People will feel less threatened and (unknowingly) become more receptive to your ideas.

Confrontation can occur when sitting across from someone because eye contact is more prominent and winds up working against you. When you know a colleague or someone in the meeting is going to "get into your face," sit next to that person rather than across from him or her. Sit where you can be seen and heard. If possible, sit at, or as close as possible to, the head of the table. Or sit to the right of someone with power and you will *share the power.* Those who occupy focal positions are perceived as leaders. One study showed a group of prospective jurors. The person who takes the end seat at a table is most likely to be selected as the foreperson of the jury.

Many successful attorneys use their awareness of nonverbal communication to evaluate their colleagues, witnesses, and members of the jury. Jo-Ellan Dimitrius, author of *Reading People* and a well-known jury consultant, has successfully predicted the behavior of thousands of jurors, witnesses, lawyers, and judges during the past fifteen years by applying her ability to read visual and oral clues. She says, "When I prepare a witness for trial, I always try to help them project the best possible image. I pay attention to personal appearance, body language, voice, and, of course, the manner in which they testify." There is a distinct difference between making the best of what we have and putting on a false front.

As Abraham Lincoln said, "You may fool all the people some of the time; you can even fool some of the people all of the time; but you can't fool all of the people all the time."

CHAPTER 4

Effective Use
of Movement

Proper movement and gestures add energy to your delivery when you are speaking to large or small groups. They build contrast and increase your power and influence when you speak. Be aware of how, why, when, and where you move. Awareness is the key to freeing yourself from unnecessary movement and is best realized by watching yourself on video. Your rhythm, stance, pace, and posture are elements that will enable you to become more powerful when speaking. Gestures and movement that contradict what is spoken are a dead giveaway. An important question to ask yourself about your movement is whether it adds or subtracts from your total effectiveness.

The best and most successful way to learn *how* to control your movement is to practice and rehearse your presentation aloud numerous times. Each time you present your information, make mental notes about what's happening with your body language as you walk and talk. The more you control your movement, the more you will control your listener's attention. By showing others you can control your body, they will see someone who is in control of his or her life and career.

When speaking to a large group, you may need to use movement depending on the layout of the audience. By using movement, you can adjust to audience seating patterns. If your audience is spread in a wide space, moving across the stage in front of your audience can increase contact. If your audience is seated in a deep space, movement through your audience can increase your impact. When walking *into* an audience, do not walk down the center aisle more than 15 feet. Walking any farther will force the front rows of your audience to physically turn around in their chairs to follow your movement, which is distracting.

Think about the last time you were at a large seminar and the presenter ran up and down the aisles. How effective was that person? Certainly not as effective as he or she could have been had the person been in control of his or her movement.

Moving in relaxed coordination with what you are saying not only engages your audience but also prevents you from stiffening, as often happens when one sits or stands in one place for too long. Examples of natural, expressive movement might include walking toward your audience when emphasizing a point, or walking away, leaving them to contemplate a question you have just posed. Make all your movements purposeful.

Movement can be used to create a more dynamic presence. By using movement when you speak, you add an extra level of energy to your delivery. It also adds highlights, builds contrast, and increases power. You can add tremendous contrast to your delivery by varying pace, direction, center of energy, and style. Use these elements in creative ways to heighten listeners' interest and involvement. Movement can be used to create interesting characters; you can add colorful highlights to characterization, particularly when you are quoting, telling a story, or sharing an anecdote.

Movement has some drawbacks and can cause problems if not used properly. It shifts focus from your face to your body. When you move, people focus on what you are doing rather than on what you are saying. Movement dominates attention and can easily overshadow a business message. Coordinate your message with your movement. When you move, random movement may feel good, but it gives the impression of nervousness. By moving at the wrong time, your message gets lost. It can be a challenge to control. When you move, be aware of *how* you are moving in addition to *where* you are moving. Unconscious rhythms and habits send unintended messages. Do not pace like a caged animal, as this would be more of a distraction than an enhancement to your information. Movement can become boring. When we move, we tend to move in a consistent pattern and rhythm. In speaking, power comes from contrast. Any consistent element—pace, gestures, movement—can become boring quickly. One way to use movement more effectively is to create contrast and build excitement. By stepping forward, stopping, and delivering a key line, you create tremendous highlights. If you are a *walker and a talker* or like to *jump on tables*, remember to *walk and talk* **only when what you are saying is a "throw-away" line or a line of transition to your next thought**. By moving on lines that are not critical points, you can use your movement, as well as your words, to add punctuation and contrast.

Another way movement can be used in a positive way is as a transitional element when summarizing key points. For example, walk across the room, stop, and summarize your information. This adds emphasize while increasing impact. Movement can be used effectively by responding to problems with your sight lines. If you cannot see your audience, they cannot see you. Movement is critical in establishing eye contact. If you don't have a place to stand where you can see everyone, you may have to become more strategic with your movement.

Your rhythm, stance, pace, posture—the more you focus on these elements, the more powerful your movement will become. Concentrate on your choices and get involved with each motion. Be aware of *what* you are doing and *how* effective your movement really is. The more you control your movements, the more you control your audience's attention. Movement is not a solution to tension; it's a strategic tool to be used to naturally enhance your information.

CHAPTER 5

Gesturing for Impact

Gestures are another way to add interest and impact when speaking. Gestures can be tremendously powerful. They should be natural, expressive, and clear. They are used to enhance your message, clarify your meaning, or emphasize an important point. Gestures must emerge naturally from within and not appear stiff, robotic, or insincere. Gesturing not only conveys meaning, but adds energy to your speaking. Just as a conductor uses a baton to synchronize the orchestra, you can employ gestures to help conduct your message to the brains of your audience.

Many people are so shy about speaking in the first place they would prefer not to call attention to themselves by moving at all when they give a presentation. Some people are not demonstrative by nature. Men typically are not as physically expressive as women. In fact, many men think a stoic delivery is a sign of masculinity and control.

You don't need to look like a windmill in a hurricane to get your point across. Just add some life to your speaking by letting your body talk as much as your mouth. Use smooth, fluid, deliberate gestures above the waist. Be expansive. Get some daylight between the waist and upper arm area. Gesturing too close to the body is distracting. Think about your own personal area of space— a *pie-shaped bubble* in front of you and to your sides. An *open-palmed* gesture with the hand moving forward at chest height, fingers up and palm out, expresses honesty and openness. Both hands open at chest level and spread sideways, palms up, signals a plea to be understood. Avoid pointing a *finger* at your audience, as this can be perceived as a reprimanding gesture.

Chest high gestures are best as they transmit strength, quiet authority, and assurance. Practice in front of a mirror. If possible, videotape yourself. Polishing your use of gestures will add credibility, confidence, and authority to your information.

In business situations, stand close enough to the other person to be personal, but not so close to be intrusive—approximately 2 to 3 feet. Let your information speak through your gestures. Rapid, jerky gestures close to the body are distracting—people begin to watch your hands and arms flailing and forget about listening to you and your information. Make sure there is daylight between your upper arm and ribcage. Relax and let your body go. Use gestures to demonstrate your passion and enthusiasm, and to release physical energy you are feeling.

Gestures improve voice quality. They help to relax the entire body, allowing the voice to become smoother and less strained. When you gesture, you physically and productively release nervous energy. This energy is what you want to be sharing with your audience. Gestures add power to your message while giving you something to do with your hands. Synchronize your words and gestures. Learning to use gestures deliberately can be a powerful way to project honesty and truth. Successful people gesture because they know it sets them apart from others who do not. Whether you are speaking one-to-one or in front of a group, by implementing natural, expressive gestures, you appear more confident, comfortable, and relaxed.

CHAPTER 6

Eye Contact

Eyes are the most important facial communicators. Looking a person straight in the eye has always signaled honesty. Eye contact is the single most powerful and influential means of communication we possess. The head and face are the most expressive parts of our body. Our faces are capable of showing pain, joy, shock, anger, surprise, exhaustion, happiness, sorrow, boredom, doubt, and more. The face can pout, frown, snarl, wince, smirk, glare, frown, and blush. The head can nod, bob, jerk, shake, duck, turn, and tilt. We send numerous messages each day using our face and head. Use of these instruments is an excellent way to enhance credibility while building rapport with our listeners.

Shifty eyes are associated with deviousness. A lack of eye contact is associated with lying. When someone is lying, the amount of eye contact is about one-third less than when someone is telling the truth. Have long, strong eye contact. Maintain approximately three to five seconds of eye contact with each person when speaking to a group, fifteen to twenty seconds when speaking one-to-one. Too much eye contact can be unsettling for some people and may be regarded as communicating superiority, lack of respect, or a wish to insult. It's not necessary to have a stare-down with a person. If you want to make people feel inadequate, simply stare at them. The long, blank look is an outright insult. If you're making someone uncomfortable with your eye contact, look at another person.

My number one pet peeve is when you meet a person for the first time and he or she gives you the "once over." They look you up and down from the top of your head to the tip of your shoes. This is rude, insulting behavior and a sure way to alienate a co-worker, customer, or potential client. If you have this nasty habit, get rid of it!

Too little eye contact is perceived as lack of interest, boredom, insecurity, dishonesty, or shyness. Lowering the eyes is taken as a signal of submission. Eye contact should be a simple, natural expression of interest you show to your audience.

Years ago, many presentation classes taught the participants to focus on an imaginary dot at the back of a room or to look over people's heads if they were at all uncomfortable or nervous when speaking to groups. This approach is no longer acceptable. Read people's faces and expressions. Talk **to** your audience, not **at** them. (Don't be a "talking head," standing there, dumping information on your listeners.) Focus on the triangular area of a person's face: from the top of the brow line to the base of the chin. Whether you choose to look at the nose, chin, lips, or eyes, as long as you stay within the triangular area of the face you will be perceived as more sincere, honest, believable, credible, and trustworthy.

For those who wear eyeglasses, avoid tinted lenses. Buy clear, nonglare lenses. You can be perceived as untrustworthy, shifty, and/or dishonest if your eyes aren't visible. People must be able to see your eyes. As mentioned in Chapter 1, people who wear eyeglasses are perceived as more intelligent and more successful. Avoid the half-glass bifocals—you may be perceived as condescending or "looking down your nose" at your audience. Order eyeglasses with a full-size lens with the bifocals across the bottom half; this creates a more natural and professional look.

Breaking eye contact

When breaking eye contact, do not look up at the ceiling or off into space or you could be perceived as uncertain, hesitant, and lacking confidence. Look off to the side or down at your notes. If you happen to lose your train of thought, look down at your notes. People will perceive you to be "thinking" about what you are going to say next—as long as your pause doesn't last more than a few seconds. Because listeners aren't used to hearing silence—many times this is when they pay attention—*they assume you are getting ready to say something important.*

In a training situation or when presenting important information, you want to be sure your audience is following along and understanding exactly what you're telling them. When you see a puzzled expression or quizzical look, pause. Ask the (confused) person directly or the entire group if there are any questions. Pause. If anyone has a question, you're allowing him or her time to think of it.

Speaking to groups

When attending a meeting or speaking to a group around a conference table and someone asks you a question, **do not** have a one-to-one conversation with the person who asked the question. Spread your eye contact around. Begin your answer with the person who asked it, then speak to the rest of the group as well. At the end of your answer, you can look back at the person who asked the question. At that point, you can ask him or her if your answer clarified the question. By remembering to use this technique, you involve everyone and no one feels slighted or left out.

When presenting (or speaking) to a large group, maintain long, strong, direct eye contact with one person in the audience; three to five seconds of eye contact with each person is a good rule of thumb. The rapport you are building with that person is spread to others in the general area in a triangular pattern. People cannot tell *exactly* where you are looking when you're speaking to a large group. They will perceive you to be looking at them, even though you may be looking at the person *in front of* or *behind* them.

Don't rapidly scan back and forth across your audience, looking like a windshield wiper in motion. Look at and see individuals in the audience as if each one were the only person in the room.

It's important to include as many people as possible in your eye contact. Look around the audience at random and pick people out; don't try to go row by row or take one side and then the other. The impression you give is that you are concerned about what you're saying and the audience finds it easy to become involved along with you. Strong, focused eye contact contributes significantly to an image that has authority, believability, and confidence.

In *Body Language in the Workplace*, Julius Fast discusses how powerful and evident the subtext sent by eye contact can be. The following example details a lawsuit that took place between two oil companies.

Pennzoil sued Texaco, claiming Texaco had improperly interfered with a deal it had with Getty Oil. Pennzoil won a damage award of **over 2.5 billion dollars plus interest**, the largest in the history of the United States.

During the trial, the Texaco lawyers thought Pennzoil's counsel were playing up to the jury by instructing their witnesses always to make eye contact with the jurors and to joke with them. In an attempt to paint a contrast, Texaco counsel instructed their witnesses to be serious and absolutely avoid looking at the jurors. The case went against Texaco.

In conversations after the verdict, the jurors said, "Those Texaco witnesses never looked at us once. They were arrogant and indifferent. How could we believe them?" Conventional legal wisdom says Texaco counsel were right in "not putting on a show for the jury." But their witnesses were so concerned with avoiding eye contact they sent out a subtext of insincerity—the very thing the lawyers were trying to avoid!

Visual aids and eye contact

When speaking to a large group and using visual aids such as slides or videos, do not turn off the lights—*dim them*. You should be able to see your audience's eyes and read their facial expressions; your audience should be able to see your face and your eyes. Many clients I work with prefer to "hide in the dark," which is not acceptable. To make the most effective impression and project a credible, *confident* presence, dim the lights but don't turn them off.

Facial expressions

Nick Jordan, author of *The Face of Feeling*, writes "research has proven the eighty muscles of the face are capable of making more than seven thousand different facial expressions." Most of us can read if someone is happy, sad, or frightened, but what about the other nuances? Do you see apprehension, shyness, curiosity, hostility, humor, or warmth? As you get better at reading these signals, you will become more successful at interpersonal communications.

Facial expressions are powerful in controlling the type and amount of communication that takes place between individuals. Do you come across as enthusiastic, energetic, and animated? Do you smile occasionally, when appropriate? Or...are you serious, scowling, and severe? Do you wrinkle or furrow your brow, frown, or grimace?

Many people, particularly business executives, freeze their faces regardless of the emotional state they are in. They believe having a *poker face* creates a strategic advantage. Sometimes it will. But often, you only gain complete credibility with an audience when they feel you are completely open and not masking anything from them. The viewer generally perceives the warmer, more vulnerable personality as being stronger and less afraid.

The smile

By having a natural smile, you are communicating you're comfortable with yourself. Learning to project a light, natural smile is important in creating a positive image. A nice, light smile immediately signals an open, friendly nature. The absence of a smile conveys just the opposite: a closed, unfriendly person. Learn to smile under pressure. Cultivate the same natural smile when you're in a tough situation as when you're at ease among friends. Not only does your smile affect others, it has a positive effect on you physically. It's a fact: You will *feel* your smile throughout the rest of your body. It makes a difference in both your mind and body. Phony smiles don't work. A true smile comes from within and a person can tell when you're faking it. Remember: Smiling is first in the brain, *then* on the face.

Energy

Energy can make up for distractions. Do you constantly grin for no apparent reason or come across as too serious or deadpan? How expressive are you? Ask for feedback the next time you make a presentation or speak at a meeting. Again, videotaping yourself is the most powerful tool you can use to find out exactly what is going on with your body language, energy level, and image.

We have the ability to raise or lower our level of energy. When appropriate, such as during a motivational presentation, bring your energy level up. If you need to be more serious or somber, lower your level of energy. Control each situation by animation, tone of voice, variety in pace, and volume. Properly focused energy comes across as positive. If your energy is up, your rate, volume, and pitch will be appropriate to the situation. Remember back to a moment when you were passionate about your subject—when you knew you were communicating effectively because you truly believed what you were saying. This is your key to success.

Various polls show that the ability to communicate well is ranked the number-one key to success by leaders in business, politics, and the professions. When you communicate with someone, it's not just the words you choose to send to the other person that make up your message. You are also sending signals about what kind of person you are by your eyes; facial expression; energy; body movement; vocal pitch, tone, volume, and intensity; commitment to your message; sense of humor; and numerous other factors.

CHAPTER 7

Body Language Signals

Body language is the eloquent message we send with our posture, stance, facial expressions, and gestures. When what we say with our body language contradicts what we say with our words, an audience believes what they see over what they hear. They take you at face value. Dr. Albert Mehrabian's study shows that 55 percent of our believability and the way we are perceived is based on our body language, which includes posture, gestures, and eye contact.

Thirty-eight percent of our believability and the way we are perceived is based on our voice, which includes inflection, rate of speech, and volume. Only 7 percent of our believability and the way we are perceived is based on our content, or the actual message we are providing to our listeners. It's the 93 percent of *how* we relay our message that's most important.

If you are uncomfortable with *who* you are, you make others uncomfortable, too. But if you can identify and use your good qualities as a person, others will want to be around you. The key to becoming more comfortable with your communication is to be consistently *you*, at your best, in all situations. No one can play *you* as well as you can.

Many clients come to me and say, "I don't want you to change me." Well, I can't change anyone and I don't want to. All I can do is help people identify and bring out their best qualities—those that communicate a positive message. I explain to each individual how

I don't want to make any dramatic changes in their personality; I don't want them to become someone they're not or come across as phony and insincere. I want them to realize they already have the ability within them to appear and feel confident and polished. They just need someone to show them *how* they can consistently be their best in all situations. One way to do this is to understand body language and the positive (or negative) impact it can have on a person's overall image and the way he or she is perceived.

When sharing ideas during a meeting, making a presentation, or having a casual conversation, the listener is sending a subtext of messages, nonverbally with facial expressions and body language. Learning to read those messages enables us to be more effective and if necessary, to modify some situations to our advantage.

Signals and their interpretations

- A brisk, erect, purposeful walk signals confidence.
- Touching the face or rubbing the nose signals lying, deceit, doubt.
- Rubbing the eyes signals doubt, disbelief.
- Scratching the neck signals doubt, uncertainty.
- Head down, peering over glasses or bifocals signals a judgmental, scrutinizing person.
- Head up, looking down on the audience signals a superior, smug, arrogant attitude.
- A bowed head signals shyness, insecurity, defeat.
- Constant head nodding or bobbing signals a person overly anxious or eager to please.
- A cocked or tilted head signals confusion, simple-mindedness **or** flirtation, seduction, vulnerability.
- Hands clasped behind the head, leaning back in a chair signals confidence, dominance, superiority, know-it-all attitude.

- Hands clasped behind the back, palm-in-palm signals authority, superiority, confidence. Stance could also be due to military background.

- Hands on the hips in an open stance signals aggressive behavior or a person who wants to appear larger. Stance could also be due to military or athletic background, signaling readiness.

- Standing with palms up, open, and outward signals openness, honesty.

- Shaking hands, palm down, signifies a dominant, aggressive handshake.

- Shaking hands, palm up, signifies a submissive handshake.

- Rubbing the palms together signals positive expectation, anticipation **or** crafty, devious behavior.

- Leaning away from a situation signals disinterest, noninvolvement, distaste.

- Hands clenched with fingers interlocked signals insecurity, frustration.

- Crossed arms at chest level signals a defensive, negative posture **or** a nervous, shy, insecure individual.

- Crossing the legs while standing signals nervousness, shyness, insecurity.

- Straddling a chair backwards signals dominance, aggression.

- Sitting with legs crossed, foot kicking slightly signals boredom, lack of interest.

- Locked ankles signals apprehension.

- Tapping or drumming fingers on a table signals impatience, boredom.

- Steepling fingers signals authority—too much can be condescending.

- Patting, fondling or touching the hair signals lack of self-confidence, insecurity.

- Stroking the arm of a chair, fingering a glass or a pen, or stroking an arm or leg sends a subtext of loneliness.
- Pulling or tugging at the ear signals indecision.

The ability to learn and recognize the elements of subtext—the body language signals that accompany our words—allows you to express yourself more effectively in the workplace and help you to better understand others. Use this knowledge wisely. Become aware of the negative signals *you* send or of the distracting habits *you* have and eliminate them from your communication style. Realize *you* are the message. Once you do this, you will become more persuasive and convincing while making a powerful, memorable impression on everyone with whom you come into contact.

CHAPTER 8

The Power of Your Voice

Another area of importance is breathing, sound, and voice. As mentioned earlier, research has shown 38 percent of our believability and the way we are perceived is based on our voice. This includes projection, inflection, articulation, and rate. Do you have strong voice projection? Is your enunciation and pronunciation clear and relaxed? How is your inflection? Would you like to become a more dynamic speaker?

The voice, like the smile, is shaped by a combination of muscles and emotions. You can improve your voice (more quickly) by working on your emotional expression than by working on mechanical drills. Your voice, like your posture, gestures, movement, and eye contact, should be natural, expressive, and clear. Our voices are much more flexible than we may think and we often have a much wider vocal range than we may realize. You can enhance your voice by recognizing and eliminating unnecessary elements in your vocal usage. In order to do this, you must first become aware of the power of the pause.

The power of the pause

The pause is an incredibly powerful technique to give your spoken image authority, energy, and audience awareness. Pauses are needed in speech to allow you to relax and breathe. This gives your voice energy, gives you time to see your audience, and in the event you get off-track, allows you to regain control of a speaking situation. The pause lends importance to the words just spoken, and thus contributes to the impression of authority. A common tendency among speakers is to fill the spaces that might otherwise be pauses/silence with *fillers*: "ahs," "uhs," "ums," and "you knows" or by clearing the throat. This need to fill up all the *empty space* detracts from authority because it communicates a fear of silence. We're all guilty of using fillers, particularly when we get caught off-guard or are searching for what we want to say. Too many fillers cause distraction, take away from credibility, and make you appear hesitant, uncertain, and unfamiliar with your topic.

A few years ago, Jonathan Demme won an Academy Award for best director of a motion picture. During his three-minute acceptance speech, he used "ah," "um," or "uh" ninety-nine times. How do I know this? The next day, an article was published on the front page of the *Minneapolis Star Tribune* about his poor delivery! Learning to pause appropriately, allowing a moment of silence, is the single most important element in making the most of your voice.

Eliminating fillers

The optimal way to eliminate fillers is to **practice reading aloud**. Ten minutes per day for a minimum of two weeks can result in a remarkable improvement and help you get rid of a *bad habit*. (If you have a serious problem, it may take longer.) Read the newspaper, a magazine, or a children's storybook. When you first begin this exercise, record your voice. Save the tape and record your voice again two weeks later. Not only will you hear a difference in your use of non-words, but you will realize your voice inflection and enunciation have greatly improved. Becoming aware of and eliminating non-words enables you to develop a more powerful, expressive speaking rhythm.

When presenting, look at your audience and speak with sincerity. Pause consciously. Don't make sentences too long. Use short, punchy phrases so you can scan your notes with your eyes and look up when delivering your information. Don't look down to read the final word of every line. Instead, quickly glance down to "scoop up" the last few words of a sentence. Pause. Look up and speak directly to the audience. Take your time. Pace your looking down and looking up so your eyes are *up* at the end of a sentence.

The average person speaks at a rate of 160 to 200 words per minute. You and your audiences' minds are racing at between 1,200 and 1,500 words per minute. Pausing gives you the opportunity to think about what you want to say next and gives you a chance to collect yourself. It also gives your audience time to digest your message and better understand what you have just told them. An appropriate pause actually creates audience interest and grabs their attention.

Silence is golden

Most people are uncomfortable with pausing and the silence it creates. The following story (from the *Speakers Sourcebook II* by Glenn Van Ekeren) is a favorite I share when coaching clients about the power of the pause.

When Western Union offered to buy Thomas Edison's newly invented ticker, Edison had no idea how much to ask for it. He asked for and was granted a few days to think about the purchase price. Edison and his wife talked about the offer. Although stunned by Mrs. Edison's suggestion to ask for twenty thousand dollars, he hesitantly agreed and set out to meet the Western Union officials.

"What price have you decided on?" the Western Union representative asked. When Edison attempted to tell him twenty thousand dollars, the figure stuck to the roof of his mouth. He stood speechless. Impatient and uncomfortable with the pending silence, the Western Union businessperson finally blurted, "How about one hundred thousand dollars?"

Silence truly is golden and Thomas Edison would no doubt agree.

Animation

For those who lack animation or just want to be more dynamic, I again suggest reading a children's book aloud using all the animation and enthusiasm you can possibly muster. Underline the important words in every sentence. Be generous with yourself but don't try to become overly exciting suddenly. Record yourself as you read and play the tape back to check your progress. You will be pleasantly surprised at how quickly this practice positively affects your speaking. Ten minutes per day is all you need.

Rate of speech

Don't talk too fast or too slow. Have variation, inflection, and intonation when speaking. Record yourself in different situations to monitor where and when you use the most fillers. Videotape—another excellent way to detect bad habits you probably aren't aware of—an upcoming presentation. Some fast talkers come from families where there is a lot of competition for the floor. Others have a genetic speed streak—they walk fast, work fast, and also talk fast. Rapid speech can be a sign of stress. When your body is feeling pressure, your bodily rhythms speed up, including speech patterns.

The good news about fast talking: Research has proven audiences prefer to listen to a person who speaks faster than slower. People who talk faster are judged to be more intelligent and credible than those who talk slower. The bad news: Speaking too fast can cause poor articulation, making you sound hurried. If you are talking so fast that people find you hard to understand or wonder why you're so eager to "get it over with," start slowing down your speech with this technique: **pause and breathe**. Rather than having to worry about reminding yourself to "slow down," just remember to pause and breathe. This technique automatically slows down and enhances your rate of speech.

Grammar

It's important to have good grammar, but if we were to transcribe each and every word, some sentences would be grammatically correct and some would not. Research has proven we make a mistake every sixteen words, whether it's with pronunciation, intonation, or word choice. We can't and won't have perfect speech, but not using proper grammar can definitely keep you from getting ahead socially as well as professionally.

Prejudices are held against those who consistently use poor grammar. Judgments are made regarding intelligence, social status, level of education, and class. (I have worked with numerous clients who have not received promotions because of their poor grammar.) In order to use English correctly and gracefully, it is necessary to recognize and practice using good grammar; self-awareness is important. Also, listening to speakers who are accustomed to speaking grammatically helps to train the ear to recognize correct usage.

Nonexistent words

From Stephen J. Manhard's *The Goof-Proofer* here are some of the most typical *nonexistent words* that are frequently misused:

Wrong	Right
Alot	A lot
Alright	All right
Analyzation	Analysis
Fer	For
Heighth	Height
Interpretate	Interpret
Irregardless	Regardless
Marshall	Marshal
Momento	Memento
Renumeration	Remuneration
Realitor	Realtor
Restauranteur	Restaurateur
Smoothe	Smooth
Unequivocably	Unequivocally

If you are guilty of any of these glaring goofs, try hard to remember "there ain't no such" words. Misusing them immediately brands you as a person whose English education has been sadly neglected. Learning proper use of grammar and refreshing your skills is not difficult and won't take you that long. Here are some ways to do this:

- Get a basic high school grammar book, study it daily, and apply what you learn each day to all conversations and communication (written and oral).

- Attend a one-day seminar where they address the important elements of good grammar. Continually work at implementing the tools and techniques suggested.

- Pay attention to your tenses and keep them consistent.

- Eliminate "gonna," "wanna," "coulda," "shoulda," and "woulda" in your speech.

Enhancing this area of your communication will be well worth the time you invest. All of us need to refresh our grammatical skills occasionally. Don't be embarrassed by having to look up a word or double-check a rule.

Stumbling over words

As much as we would like to think so, our listeners are not hanging on our every word. If you make a mistake, let it go. Remember: Our minds are racing at a rate of 1,200 to 1,500 words per minute, but we only speak at a rate of 160 to 200 words per minute. Repeat or repronounce a word if you must, but do not let it negatively affect your presentation or the way you deliver your information.

Your audience is mentally drifting in and out. They may not even notice your error. If you've lost your place or blanked out, **say nothing**. Don't whack yourself along side the head or roll your eyes toward the ceiling. After you have taken a breath, continue on. There's a very good chance no one noticed your temporary lapse.

Never apologize or say "I'm sorry" when presenting. Apologizing reduces credibility and makes you appear unsure and timid. It's rare to hear a newscaster apologize for making a mistake;

pay attention to this when listening to the news. If you need to say "excuse me" and repeat a word or restate a sentence, do so.

Start each new thought or sentence with a new breath of air and save enough breath, or take another breath mid-sentence, to finish your thought with power. Many presenters have a tendency to run out of air at the end of a sentence and forget to properly breathe at that time. Pausing and taking a breath enables you to begin your next sentence with strong voice projection while enhancing your inflection. Practice the power of the pause and you will feel the positive difference it makes in all of your communication.

Relaxed breathing

By learning to breathe properly, you will feel less tense and appear more relaxed. It is one of the most effective ways to control sweaty palms, a racing or pounding heart, a quivering voice, or butterflies in your stomach. The number-one mistake people make when they breathe is to use their upper chest instead of their abdominal muscles. The term "diaphragmatic breathing" is a popular misconception. The diaphragm, which is a thin membrane located beneath the lungs separating the lungs from the stomach and the intestines, does not breathe. The abdominal muscles are the most important for breathing.

Place your hand on your midriff and breathe—you can feel these muscles operating like a bellows. The mouth and nose are coordinated with the diaphragm and abdominal muscles. This co-ordination is all that's needed for steady, peaceful breathing. It is the foundation of good sound that helps relax the entire body when we feel tense or nervous. Dogs, cats, and babies all use their abdominal muscles when they breathe. When we sleep and are completely relaxed, we use our abdominal muscles to breathe. During the day, when stressful situations occur, we tighten the upper chest and throat, creating tension. This can be very damaging to our vocal cords because we are putting additional strain on them.

Large amounts of air do not need to be taken in when breathing. More air does not necessarily mean more power to your voice.

When feeling tense or nervous, you take in air in shallow breaths and do not release it as frequently as you should. Carbon dioxide builds up, increasing your anxiety. Some people get headaches. The normal breathing cycle takes in oxygen, then lets carbon dioxide out. In order for your body to function properly, this needs to happen.

Some religions, such as Buddhism and Hinduism, use breath control as a key to inner peace and tranquillity. Breathing is used to obtain a higher level of consciousness. The long life span in many of the yogis in India and the Himalayas attests to this technique.

A shakiness or quiver in the voice can be caused by feeling tense but is most likely caused by lack of air and improper breathing. Most of us don't breathe as deeply or as slowly as we should, especially when feeling uncomfortable. Pause and breathe while having a moment of silence; this eliminates the shakiness. As mentioned earlier, it also allows your thoughts to catch up with what you want to say next and enables your listeners to process what you have just told them.

A few years ago, I worked with a woman who "hummed" at the end of her sentences. (Yes, "hummed.") She had missed out on numerous opportunities for promotion and job satisfaction due to her peculiarity. It diminished all credibility and professionalism in the minds of everyone she worked with. Our first step was to address her overall communication style—then we analyzed her breathing (or lack of it). Her "humming" was caused by improper breathing and lack of air when she became anxious or nervous. After numerous sessions, she was able to breathe in a more relaxed manner when stressed, which eliminated most of her "humming." She has since been promoted twice.

There are numerous benefits to properly breathing. When using your chest to breathe, which is what you *don't* want to do, your chest rises, your stomach pulls in, your shoulders raise and pull back, and you often hear your breath. When you breathe out, your chest lowers, your stomach releases, your shoulders drop, you often hear your breath, and you feel a sense of release and relaxation.

When using your abdominal muscles to breathe, your chest does not rise, your stomach releases, your shoulders remain lowered, you do not hear your breath, and you feel a sense of relaxation. When you breathe out, your chest does not rise, your stomach pulls in, your shoulders remain lowered, you do not hear your breath, and you feel a sense of control. This is exactly opposite of what you're used to. Chest breathing is an *unconscious* effort; abdominal breathing is a *conscious* effort, which will take some practice.

Breathing exercise

Here is a breathing exercise to help you to learn how to control your breath. Wear nonconfining clothing during this exercise.

1. Lie on your back on the floor, a couch, or a firm mattress.

2. Place one hand on your abdominal muscles and one hand on your chest.

3. Breathe in slowly through your nose. Expand your stomach as if it were a balloon. The hand on your chest should not move.

4. Exhale through your mouth. Your abdomen should sink in. Keep trying until it does. Do not move your chest.

5. Repeat steps 1 through 4, counting silently as you go. Take in as much air as possible. When you have reached your limit, press in with your palms in order to push out the air that is left.

6. Repeat step 5. This time, push your stomach up toward the ceiling, as you let out a loud, strong "AH." Keep your throat open.

7. Work toward four *slow* counts on the inhale; eight *slow* counts on the exhale.

8. When this is mastered, and only then, try doing it sitting up and eventually when standing.

Concentrate on:

- Making sure your abdominal muscles are moving in the right direction.
- Regulating your counts.
- Keeping your throat and jaw relaxed at all times.

Proper breathing increases the flow of oxygen to the brain. It relaxes tense muscles and reduces nervousness and anxiety. Along with this, your voice quality improves and your facial muscles appear more natural and relaxed. You can use abdominal breathing anytime, anywhere—while you are waiting to speak, when your mind goes blank, while you are listening, during a meeting or interview, or when you are sitting in traffic in your car. The next time someone cuts you off on the highway, don't "gesture" at the person, remind yourself to take a couple of deep breaths and relax. The benefits of abdominal breathing are numerous. It **does** require a conscious effort, but it helps produce a more relaxed sound that enables you to establish a sense of power and control. It also helps establish an even rhythm, giving you added ease and composure while delivering your message.

In her book, *Talk to Win*, Dr. Lillian Glass discusses how she has introduced the tension blow-out technique explained below to prisoners in federal and state penitentiaries in California. She has received reports from the wardens that "the technique effectively helps the prison inmates reduce their stress and anxiety and release their anger." When feeling tense or angry:

1. Take a breath in through your mouth for three seconds.
2. Hold it for three seconds.
3. Blow out air until you have no air left. Keep pushing until you are completely out of air. Pretend you are blowing up a balloon.
4. Do not breathe for three seconds.
5. Now breathe in for three seconds and repeat steps 1 through 4 three times. Afterward, proceed to breathe normally. You may

feel a bit light-headed; don't worry as this will go away. You should feel much better and less angry. If you're still angry, repeat this exercise.

Think of your chest as a bagpipe that you fill to the point of bursting. Your lung full of air is ready to be used for effective speaking. You control it. It relieves the tension in your body, yet keeps you alert. It's the same principle used for Lamaze breathing as taught to expectant mothers in birthing classes. Yoga creates relaxation and power. These exercises increase physical stamina and keep your brain energized.

For anyone who plays golf and utilizes abdominal breathing, yardage is increased when hitting off the tee or out of the fairway. (Your ball may not go any straighter and you may still hook or slice, but it will go farther.) I once coached a gentleman who didn't believe this theory. He immediately went out, tried it, and increased his yardage off the tee by over 60 yards! Needless to say, he was shocked. Whether you play tennis, jog, walk, ski, skate, or box, all sport enthusiasts will increase their stamina and derive positive benefits by consciously relaxing their breathing.

Pitch

If you must ask people several times what they're saying before you finally understand them, the problem is often one of pitch, or how high or low the voice is. We ordinarily end sentences with a drop in pitch (downward inflection) and end questions with a rise in pitch (upward inflection). Downward inflection makes your words sound definite, confident, and persuasive. Most phrases and sentences should end with definite downward inflections. In other words, use your voice to put periods at the ends of sentences. Upward inflections—the tilt or lilt to a higher pitch at the end of a word or toward the end of a sentence—carry the sound and sense of a question, as if you are unsure of yourself and a little scared. Upward inflections compromise your authority and take away from your influence.

People consider a lower pitch more authoritative and influential. Men naturally have a lower pitch. A low pitch carries conviction and authority, which is why a woman should make every attempt to speak in strong, low tones. Does the tone of your voice send out a different message than your words? Concentrate on using downward inflection. Practice with a tape recorder. Notice the difference and be conscious of the signals your voice transmits.

Nasality

Talking through your nose makes everything you say sound as if you are complaining or whining. Listening to someone with a whiny voice grates on our nerves so much we do not even want to hear what the person has to say. Research has shown that we harbor the most disdain and prejudice against people who whine.

In some cases, nasality results from a physical problem, such as a hearing impairment (that prevents effective monitoring of voice quality) or a cleft palate. It can also be due to general physical tension or by improperly talking through your nose. The voice is most nasal when it produces words that contain difficult consonants and consonant combinations; a phrase like "double indemnity" is likely to come out very nasal.

Make a list of words that contain difficult consonants, such as n, l, or v, and record them, speaking with your ears covered. Open everything up. Yawn, relax the jaw and the back of your throat. By holding the back of the throat open, there will be no vibration in the nasal cavity. Concentrate on opening the mouth and forming the words with the lips, exaggerating the articulation. Let the words pour out of the mouth rather than the nose. Repeat the words until they sound clear inside the head. Then take your hands away and listen to the change.

Volume

With energetic articulation and implementation of the abdominal breathing techniques discussed, you should have sufficient volume for any situation. A slow, soft voice suggests low energy, low enthusiasm, weariness, and powerlessness. To increase your volume, increase the amount of air in the lungs. Volume comes from breath support in the abdomen and not from tight throat muscles. By using your abdominal muscles to project your voice, you become more powerful during your interactions with other people. A slow, soft voice does not strengthen credibility. A full, rich resonant voice enables you to come across more believably, credibly, and confidently.

Monotone

A monotonous, boring voice is tedious to the ear. It puts your audience to sleep. People will tune you out if you have no variation to your pitch, vibration, and modulation. People who speak in a monotone voice are often unsure of themselves. We doubt their credibility and find them dull and lifeless.

You can easily change the meaning of your words and monotony in your voice, simply by varying your tone. Intonation involves the rise and fall of your voice. As discussed earlier, practice reading children's books aloud and you will be able to hear the difference. The best way to improve the vitality of your speaking ability is to take a risk and let your feelings show. Projecting those feelings is hard, but when you vary your pace, pitch, and volume, your emotional tone varies as well.

Another study done by Dr. Albert Mehrabian shows your voice—the intonation, resonance, or auditory delivery of your message—counts for as much as 84 percent of your emotional impact and believability *when people can't see you*, such as when you are talking on the telephone.

Remember...you have only **seven seconds** to make a first impression on the telephone. The important thing to remember about vocal images is they can be improved. Learning to breathe and to open the throat properly alleviates many of the problems. Strengthening your vocal image is a sure way to maximize the way others respond to you.

Voice mail that gets results

You are tied up all day in meeting after meeting. During your lunch break, you call to check your voice mail and have fourteen messages. The first caller rambles aimlessly for what seems like hours. Your tendency may be to skip to the end of the message or save it to listen to later, but it's a customer and you need to know why he or she is calling. You are forced to painstakingly listen to the message, rewinding it several times, trying to write down all the relevant details. Such a waste of precious time.

Poorly executed voice mail often gets in the way of effective business communication. The problem is that many business people launch into rambling monologues without regard for whom they are addressing or what benefit the information has for the recipient.

Do others perceive the way you communicate as a waste of time or as valuable interaction? Do people fast forward or delete your message before listening to it because they dread it to be another "novel"? Do you take the time to play back your message or do you hurriedly leave your message, not caring *how* you are perceived? Be brief. Be organized. Be specific. An effective voice mail should include a succinct subject, point of view, and desired benefit to the listener.

Here are some specific areas to consider when developing voice mail messages that are direct and to the point:

• **Keep your message brief.** Voice mail messages should be brief, clear, and concise— twenty to thirty seconds is optimum. If your message extends for more than one minute, consider an alternative means of delivery such as email or fax. Limit yourself to one subject per message; if the recipient has to forward the message to other users, he or she can do it without having to edit extraneous material.

• **Consider the recipient.** Always consider your audience and what information is relevant and interesting to them, particularly when leaving voice mail messages with customers or prospective customers. When sending the same message to a group of people, avoid long recipient lists by prefacing your message with a group name, for example, "to the Minneapolis Branch of Customer Service Representatives."

• **Make the message appropriate.** Messages containing lots of detailed, complex information are probably more suitable for emails or memos. **Never send negative messages via voice mail.** Such messages can be perceived as harsh and have a stronger impact than you intend, particularly if the recipient replays it or forwards it to a third party. Do not abuse the urgent message option; use only in cases where immediate review is critical.

• **Check your voice quality.** Vary your pitch and volume. Occasionally, stand up when leaving a message to vary the sound of your delivery. Your vocal tones account for 84 percent of your impact on the telephone. Speak clearly and enunciate properly. Be enthusiastic. Your energy and excitement can be contagious, even over the telephone.

• **Listen to your message.** If possible, review your recorded message before sending it. Make sure there are no *filler words* or distracting rambling. If necessary, re-record the message and listen again until you get it right. **Never use a speaker phone with voice mail**—it decreases the message's audio clarity and distances you from your recipient; you will sound as if you are speaking from a barrel. Cellular telephones also cause clarity concerns.

• **Be organized.** Take a few moments to jot down your message and benefit to the recipient before launching into your message. By preparing ahead of time, you keep to the point and avoid extraneous material. Say only what you need to say and hang up. Long, drawn-out messages are annoying.

• **Be specific.** Provide enough detail to allow the recipient of your message to take your recommended action. Avoid vague expressions. Replace them with specific times and dates. Spell out unfamiliar or difficult names and avoid all industry jargon to maximize listener understanding. **Always leave your telephone number**, including your extension, if you have one. If this is your first call to this person or if you are not at your regular office number, repeat the telephone number you are calling from, **slowly**, so the person has time to write it down.

• **Remember** you only have one chance to make a first impression. On the telephone, your recipient has formed his or her first impression of you at **seven seconds**. Make *your* impression memorable and positive by sticking to the facts.

CHAPTER 9

Listening Techniques

Proper listening etiquette includes responding with appropriate facial expression and body movements. Lean forward, move closer, be attentive, and show interest. Use your eyes and lips to let the person know that you are listening to him or her. Smile, frown, and use your facial animation to convey what you have heard.

According to listening experts like Dr. Lyman K. Steil of the University of Minnesota, Americans spend 9 percent of the time they devote to communication each day in writing, 16 percent in reading, 30 percent in speaking, and 45 percent in listening.

Most people, however, are inefficient listeners. Tests indicate that right after listening to a ten-minute oral presentation, the average listener has heard, comprehended, accurately evaluated, and retained about half of what was said. Within forty-eight hours, retention drops another 50 percent to a 25 percent effectiveness level. By the end of a week, the retention level goes down to about 5 percent or less unless cued by something later on.

Up to 80 percent of a spoken message gets lost or garbled by the time it travels from the executive level to the sales level of a company. To quote from Dr. Steil's findings as reported by Sperry Corporation, "With more than one hundred million workers in America, a simple ten dollar listening mistake by each of them would cost a billion dollars. Letters have to be retyped, appointments rescheduled, shipments reshipped."

At one of New England Telephone's twelve divisions, it was found that 20 percent of its operator-assisted calls were delayed by listening problems. The average delay was just fifteen seconds, but cost the division 874,800 dollars a year. New England Telephone estimated it recovered about 500,000 dollars of that loss after it developed a program to teach effective listening.

The following skills are just a few examples of some ways you can sharpen your listening techniques.

Attending skills

- Facing the other person squarely with your right shoulder to the other's left shoulder helps communicate your involvement.
- Maintain a relaxed yet alert, open posture with arms and legs uncrossed.
- Position yourself at an appropriate distance from the speaker.
- Be actively involved in the conversation.
- Minimize distracting motions and gestures.
- Maintain effective eye contact. Do not stare or dart your eyes away.
- Acknowledge the other person nonverbally with head nods, smiles, and so forth.
- Lean slightly toward the person instead of sitting stiffly upright or slouching back in your chair.
- Use gestures, especially when responding, but avoid dramatic hand-waving or playing with pencils, or jabbing your finger at the person.
- Nod your head and smile.
- Cut environmental distractions to the minimum.
- Remove sizable physical barriers such as a desk or large table.
- Consciously work at attending.

People tend to think of communication as a verbal process. Experts are convinced, however, most communication is nonverbal. The most commonly quoted estimate, based on research, is that up to 93 percent of our communication is nonverbal, so attending—the nonverbal part of listening—is a basic building block of the listening process.

Following skills

These skills foster effective listening: door openers, minimal encourages, open questions, and attentive silence. Door openers are statements or questions setting the stage for the type of atmosphere that will exist during the discussion. They also encourage the other person to be more open and candid. Do the following to use door openers effectively:

- Describe the other person's body language with statements such as, "You look excited about something" or "You seem frustrated."
- Offer a nonthreatening invitation to talk.
- Use brief encounters to initiate a conversation.
- Ask one question at a time.
- Allow time for the person to fully answer your question.

Simple responses that encourage the speaker to tell his or her story are called minimal encourages. Minimal encourages are brief indicators to other persons that you are with them. They do not imply either agreement or disagreement with what the speaker said. Rather, minimal encourages let the other person know he or she has been heard and the listener will try to follow the speaker's meaning if he or she chooses to continue. Minimal encourages include the following:

- Verbal invitations such as "mm-hmm."
- Brief responses such as,
    - "Tell me more."
    - "Oh?"
    - "For instance?"
    - "Then what happened?"
    - "Really?"

–"I see."

–"Right."

Open questions, such as the following provide space for the speaker to explore his or her thoughts without being hemmed in too much by the listener's categories:

• Begin a question with who, what, when, why, or how.

• Avoid stringing questions together.

• Avoid playing "twenty questions" or sounding as if you are interrogating your interlocutor.

• Be sensitive to the other person's signs of defensiveness.

Attentive silence frees the speaker to think, feel, and express him- or herself. **Most listeners talk too much**. During the pauses in an interaction, a good listener does the following:

• Attends to the other. His or her body posture demonstrates he or she is really there for the other person.

• Observes the other. He or she see the speaker's eyes, facial expressions, posture, and gestures are all communicating. When not distracted by the other's words, he or she may "hear" body language more clearly.

• Thinks about what the other is communicating. He or she ponders what the other has said. The listener wonders what the speaker is feeling and considers the variety of responses he or she might make, then selects the one that would be most facilitative.

• When busy doing these things, the listener does not have time to become anxious about the silence.

• Never interrupts. Interrupting stops the listening and evaluation process and is the worst kind of rudeness.

Reflecting skills

Reflecting skills fall into four categories:

1. Paraphrasing.
2. Reflecting feelings.

3. Reflecting meanings.
4. Summative reflections.

Paraphrasing gives the other person an opportunity to hear his or her message stated in different words and lets him or her know how well you understood it. In addition:

- A good paraphrase is concise.
- An effective paraphrase reflects on the essentials of the speaker's message.
- A paraphrase focuses on the content of the speaker's message.
- An effective paraphrase is stated in the listener's own words.

Reflective feelings lets the other person know you are sensitive to his or her feelings. The reflection of feelings involves mirroring back to the speaker, in succinct statements, the emotions which he or she is communicating. You are then able to move toward a solution to the problem. Concentrate on these areas:

- Focus on the feeling words.
- Note the general content of the message.
- Observe the body language.
- Ask yourself, "If I were having that experience, what would I be feeling?"

When feelings and facts are joined in one succinct response, we have a reflection of meaning. Feelings are often triggered by specific events. Once a person knows how to reflect feeling and content separately, it is relatively easy to put the two together into a reflection of the meaning. This is usually best when it is honed to a single succinct sentence. The shorter the better. A rambling response impedes communication.

Summative reflections communicate your overall understanding of the message and also helps both of you balance the rest of your discussion. It is a brief restatement of the main themes and feelings the speaker expressed over a longer period of conversation than would be covered by any of the other reflective skills.

- A good summation should enable the other to speak in more depth, with clearer directionality and/or greater coherence.

- A good summary often helps the speaker understand the situation more clearly even though it is a recap of what was already said.

- An effective summary can tie the loose strands of a conversation together at its conclusion.

To use your reflecting skills effectively:

Restate in your own words the message you just heard: "What I hear you saying is..." or "In other words, you're saying...."

- Reflect only the key content or points of the message.

- State your perception of your interlocutor's feelings: "You seem angry about...."

- Pay attention to his or her nonverbal signs.

- Use empathy. Be understanding.

- Restate the main themes and feelings expressed over a longer portion of the discussion: "Let me take a few minutes to recap what we have discussed so far...."

- Use summarizing to bring a part of the conversation to a close: "Before we go on to the next item on the agenda, let's summarize what we've talked about so far...."

- Use it as a bridge to the next topic of conversation.

- Avoid expressing either approval or disapproval of the person's feelings. Feelings are fact to the other person. Avoid saying "You have a right to be angry" or "You shouldn't get so upset."

- Listen for words expressing direct feeling such as "This really burns me up" or implied feeling such as "He should have known better than that."

- Ask yourself how you would feel in the other person's shoes.

One additional critical note: It is important to use these reflecting skills when you are about to engage in a conversation with someone with whom you are going to disagree. When you disagree, the person often feels you did not listen. If you had listened, how could you possibly have disagreed? The fact is that people do disagree. However, if you do not acknowledge the content and feeling of their expressed viewpoint, the other person will not listen to you in return.

To listen, remember:

- It often shows a fine command of the language to say nothing.
- An open mind is the key to communication.
- When your mind wanders away from the moment at hand, your communication skills are bound to follow. Pay attention.
- Developing a routine will help relieve the stress of having to remember.
- Often, our inability to relax makes others nervous.
- We are each blessed with two ears and one mouth—a constant reminder we should listen twice as much as we talk.
- Finishing statements for others will diminish their desire to communicate with you.
- There is no greater compliment than demonstrating interest in another human being.
- Get out from behind your desk, take three steps beyond your office door, and you have found it: common ground.
- Ask questions...not for the sake of having something to say, but for the desire to understand.
- Listen **to** context and **for** content, and you will listen effectively.
- Is your comment pertinent? Is your comment informative? Do you have your thoughts in order? If not, you are better off listening.
- Most of us know how to keep silent but few of us know when.
- Too many meetings are a clear sign a company is in trouble.
- The key to any suggested program is "commitment" from the top executive.

Eliminate negatives

The six common barriers to communicating better are:

1. Hearing what you expect to hear. We have a tendency to selectively listen for only those things that meet our expectations. We screen out everything else. This is why different people with different expectations hear different messages from the same speech. This is why politicians are intentionally vague—they can meet everyone's expectations.

2. Evaluating the source. Have your ever received an incorrect piece of information from someone and labeled your source as "unreliable"? However, when information comes from someone with an outstanding reputation, you feel the information cannot be questioned. In other words, you evaluate the source of the information to determine its value.

3. Having different perceptions. Not everyone is like you. If you assume all people see the world as you do, you are likely to be wrong about three quarters of the time.

4. Having different intentions. When we see a person behaving or communicating a certain way, we automatically read an intention in their actions. However, people communicate in a way that's most comfortable to them.

5. Ignoring nonverbal communications. Be aware of the nonverbal signals people send when communicating but also realize that not all nonverbal signals are accurately interpreted. One needs to be sensitive to both the verbal and nonverbal messages being sent and to their meaning.

6. Being distracted by noise. Do you concentrate and communicate effectively when there is noise around? Doubtful. To be able to send and receive messages more effectively, it is preferable to find a quiet place to conduct business.

Remember that effective communication between two people exists when the receiver interprets the sender's message the way it was intended by the sender. In general, you should strive to listen 60 to 70 percent of the time and talk 30 to 40 percent. The moral: If most of the time you talk more than you listen, you are probably failing in your communication, and you are probably boring people, too.

CHAPTER 10

Handling Challenging Questions, Difficult Situations, Thinking On Your Feet

When you find yourself in a challenging or difficult situation, you must remember to stay in control. Remain unemotional and treat the person asking you a question with dignity and respect. Here are five basic steps for success in responding to questions and becoming more effective when *thinking on your feet*:

1. Listen. Look directly at the person and pay attention to what is being said. Do not allow your mind to race ahead and start thinking about your answer before you have heard the entire question.

2. Pause to organize your thoughts. Be silent. Breathe. (If you hold your breath, you will sound nervous.) This is the single most important technique you can use to become more effective. It enables you to organize your thoughts and gives your brain the few seconds it needs to find the appropriate information to be able to respond to the question.

3. Repeat the question or sum up the question by paraphrasing. This will buy you some additional time as well as improve the overall communication of the situation by clarifying the question.

4. Give a response rather than just an answer, then add one piece

of support to the answer and **stop**. Most of the time you will satisfy the seeker, so you can move on to the next topic. If you wish to say more, build in a clue word such as *main, major,* or *primary* to your response. If the seeker wants more information, a follow-up question will be asked. **Note:** Giving one main item of support is a good rule of thumb and a reminder to people *not* to give a speech.

5. Stop. Don't end your answer on an excuse. This step is vital if you want to appear more assertive and confident. Many people have a tendency to blow their credibility after they have given a good response by babbling on beyond the finish or shrugging at the end. If you cannot figure out a way to stop, repeat the essence of the question as a close: "*So that's why we decided to stop the project.*"

Hostile and challenging questions

Acknowledge the person asking the question by maintaining strong eye contact with *while he or she is asking you the question.* Break eye contact with the person *after* he or she has asked the question. This technique enables you to stay in control of the situation. State to the entire audience one of the following options:

• "The issue is..."
• "The question has been asked..."
• "The concern has been raised..."

Then restate the issue, question, or concern that was asked. This allows you additional time to think on your feet and gives your entire audience a chance to hear the question. After acknowledging a question from a hostile or challenging audience member, remember to **break eye contact with him or her and respond to the entire audience. Do not look back at the person unless you want to allow him or her an opportunity to ask you another question or "get in your face."** Remain unemotional.

Answer the individual's issue, question, or concern by giving a direct and brief answer. Continue on with your presentation after answering him or her. If the question **was not** a hostile or challenging question, you may look back at the person and, when appropriate (such as in a training class), ask him or her if you clarified the question.

Handling tough situations

- Always offer to meet with the person (who's asking too many questions) during the next break. Many times, the person constantly interrupting you just wants to hear him- or herself speak and is attempting to monopolize or take over your presentation. He or she usually won't bother to meet with you afterwards because there is no longer an audience.

- Do not make up answers or lie if you are not sure of the answer. Ask the person to meet with you during the next break and you will find out the correct answer. Better yet, have the person write the question on the back of his or her business card. This will provide you with all the information you need. Get back to the person the same day or within a maximum of twenty-four hours.

- If you know someone in the audience can answer a question you cannot, repeat the question to that person. (Always repeat the question in case he or she was not paying attention or listening. You never want to embarrass anyone in front of his or her peers or subordinates.) Be careful with this technique, you must have solid rapport with the person.

- The more challenging the question, the shorter your answer should be.

- Use an *open palm* to point at a person asking a question rather than using your *finger*, which is considered a reprimanding gesture.

- **Never say:** "Great question!" or "I'm so glad you asked that question!" unless you can compliment every person asking questions. This eliminates the possibility of (unintentionally) offending someone in the audience.

- Do not refer to the person asking the question by name unless you are prepared to call on everyone else in the audience by name.

- When speaking with the media be friendly, brief, direct, and positive. Stay composed and unemotional at all times.

Preparing for questions

- Write down three or four basic questions you answer frequently. These are apt to be questions about your basic service or product or your organization or business.

- Practice a response—the answer, plus one main piece of support for each question.

- Build in a clue so you can establish a conversation rather than give a closed response to the question.

- Here are five ways to get a better question to respond to:

  1. Ask to have the question repeated.

  2. Ask a question of your own.

  3. Ask for clarification.

  4. Ask for a definition.

  5. Clarify or define a point yourself.

Types of situations

There are numerous types of interruptions and challenges that may arise when dealing with diverse audiences. Some of the most common are:

Preconditions

"You said exactly the same thing last year but we didn't achieve it. How are we going to achieve it this year?" Diffusion: "The issue is how this year's plan is achievable. The main reason why this year's plan is achievable is because our customer's requirements have changed significantly." At that point, give a couple of sound examples about how your customer's requirements have changed and then continue on with your information.

Agreement with a negative

"Don't you agree your plan has too many loopholes?" Diffusion: "The issue has been raised regarding the thoroughness of our plan; we have examined the situation from many perspectives." Give a few examples of how the situation was examined and why your plan is the best option.

Trigger words

"How can you possibly implement a program that's going to **rape** the environment?" Diffusion: "The concern has been raised regarding what **impact** this program will have on the environment. To determine environmental impact, we have conducted several independent studies." This can be a difficult situation. Pause and breathe for a moment, restate the question, and turn the negative question into a more positive one. If possible, state positive impacts the program will have on the environment.

Tone of voice

"How much money do you need now?" (May be whiny.) This person could be seeking straightforward information but is delivering it in an insulting tone. Remember to remain unemotional and to treat the person asking you the question with dignity and respect. Rephrase his or her concern, address it, and continue on.

Types of people

There are numerous types of people we must deal with on a daily basis. Some of the most common include:

Difficult people

A person whose behavior causes difficulties for you and others is a difficult person. Dealing with difficult people simply means dealing with difficult behaviors. This involves learning how to manage your side of a two-way transaction. For example, a client starts to berate you for something that was not your fault. Your natural reaction might be to defend yourself. Most of us have a tendency to respond this way; however, you rarely solve anything by being defensive. Another reaction might be that you're furious but grit your teeth, having allowed the situation to get to you. Ask yourself, "Is the client mad at me or the situation?" In most cases, it's the situation. Before responding to any type of difficult situation, take time to recognize the client is not angry at you. Therefore, there is no need to defend yourself, which is the best solution.

You can concentrate on solving the client's problem, making it a win-win situation for everyone involved. Focus on your client's problem rather than on your own feelings. At this point, you want to listen, ask questions, and take notes. Make sure you have your own act together before tackling difficult people. You're in charge of making the choice on how to react in difficult situations. Take control. If you allow someone else to upset you, you lose control.

Emotional people

When dealing with emotional people, remain calm and listen. Let the person talk because some of the emotion will be resolved through talk. You can't solve the problem as long as the person is emotional. You must be patient and tolerant and allow the person to respond in his or her own way.

Explosive people

You cannot use logic with an irrational, explosive person. **Never** argue with an angry person, because people tend **not** to rage if they have no one with whom to do so. Remain calm and use silence as a verbal strategy. When the angry person finally realizes he or she is the only one exploding, the fireworks will end. You don't have to avoid the person, just ignore the explosion. Another element to keep in mind about some explosive people is that they are bullies who enjoy the drama of the moment. Respond by saying, "I know you're angry, but I'm asking you to lower your voice and be objective." If the person's voice starts to rise, raise your hand to indicate *stop* and say, "I object to this behavior."

We're all human and vulnerable. Speakers succeed *only if* their audience allows them to. This happens when the speaker sincerely tries to communicate with the audience, as opposed to acting full of self-importance. Audiences respond more favorably to a speaker who remains unemotional and treats every individual asking a question with dignity and respect.

CHAPTER 11

Business and Dining Etiquette

Most people invite others to lunch in order to develop or maintain business or personal relationships. In these social situations, your table manners say a lot about you and the way you conduct business. They demonstrate the attention to detail that should be an integral part of the philosophy of anyone who wants to achieve and maintain a competitive edge. People with good manners treat others with respect. Knowing the rules is one thing. Handling yourself in a proper way during business and social situations is another. Many second and third job interviews are scheduled around a meal.

The following is a brief overview regarding etiquette. If you are at all concerned about any of these areas, I suggest you invest in a good book. I recommend *Complete Guide to Executive Manners* by Letticia Baldridge.

- If you are the first to be seated when meeting someone in a restaurant, wait until everyone has arrived before ordering a beverage. Ordering a "double scotch on the rocks" is not recommended.

- Wait for everyone at the table to be served before you begin eating.

- Maintain the same pace of eating as the person with whom you are dining. If the person is a slow eater, expand on a mutually interesting topic while he or she is eating. If you are a slow eater, ask the person a question that might take a few minutes to answer.

- Do not break crackers into your soup. When crackers are served, break off a small portion and place the remaining cracker on the underplate.

- Place your napkin in your lap as soon as everyone has been seated. No, you do not want to tuck it into the neck of your shirt to protect your tie. If you have a tendency to "wear" your food, eat slowly and carefully. When everyone at the table has finished eating and drinking, the napkin is placed to the right of the place setting.

- When the napkin is placed in a goblet, it is usually best to wait for the server to present it to you. Your napkin stays on your lap until everyone has finished eating and drinking. It is then placed to the right of the place setting. Wadding it up into a ball is uncouth.

- If someone asks for the salt, **pass both** the salt and pepper together.

- Each time you're served, unless you are involved in conversation and do not want to break eye contact, it's recommended you acknowledge the server. Forms of thanks include a verbal thank you, a smile, or even a nod. Gushing with gratitude is not necessary.

- Remember to keep solids to your left, liquids to your right. What if the person seated next to you doesn't realize he or she has just placed his or her roll on your bread plate? One solution is to thank the person for the roll. (You can be sure the etiquette offender will not use your bread plate again.) Another solution is to use the bread and butter plate to your right, thus causing everyone at the table to use the wrong plates. Or you can discretely ask your server for a bread and butter plate. If nothing else, you can simply forego having a roll and realize that, after all, this is not your last supper.

- Pass food to the right. Food should be passed counterclock-wise. This procedure supports the seating etiquette rule: Your guest should **always** be seated to your right.

- When dining with colleagues and you're beginning to pass the "community" food, you may offer it to the person on your left, help yourself, then proceed to pass it to your right.

- Allow food that has been preordered to be served to you even if you know you won't like it. Let's say you are attending a banquet and can see from what is being served to the other guests that you are not going to like the soup. Even if you abhor clam chowder, allow it to be served to you. By doing so, you ensure those around you feel comfortable as they begin the course. To look as if you are participating, lay your soup spoon in the soup bowl or on the service plate.

- Do not stack your dishes, either while you are eating or when you have finished.

- When you have finished eating, place your fork, knife, and other utensils used at the clock position of ten minutes to four, with the base of the utensils at the four and the sharp ends pointing to ten.

- When presented with a finger bowl at the end of the meal, don't dip your napkin in the bowl and wipe off your mouth. The finger bowl is for your fingers only. If you are presented with a warm, damp cloth, the same rule applies.

- Don't use your fingers to push food onto your fork; if neces-sary, use a small piece of bread. Refrain from "sopping" your gravy with your bread.

- When serving yourself butter, put the amount you will need on your butter or salad plate. Do not hold up the passing by taking the butter directly from the dish and buttering your bread. With potatoes, the same rule applies: Take a pat of butter and put it on your butter plate or directly on your potato.

- The butter knife, when not being used, should be placed diagonally or horizontally at the top of the bread plate. Break the bread into three or four pieces before buttering and eating—**don't butter the entire roll**.

- If your soup is too hot to eat, never blow on it, stir it, or drop an ice cube into it.

- Toothpicks should not be used at the table; wait until you leave. If you are bothered by food stuck between your teeth, excuse yourself and go to the restroom to remove it. Whatever you do, **don't pick the food out with your fingers**.

- If you want to taste someone else's food, pass him or her your fork **or** ask him or her to put some of their food on the corner of your plate.

- When time is of the essence, begin business discussions **after** you have ordered.

- If business is to be discussed after lunch, an alcoholic beverage should not be consumed. For business dinners, use your good judgment. Whatever the business situation, do not allow your drink to speak for you. If you order a mixed drink, use the "stirrer" for stirring, not as a mini-straw.

- If you're drinking beer, always request a glass.

- When serving red wine, fill an 8-ounce glass approximately half way. This allows the bouquet of the wine to expand. When serving white wine, fill it three-quarters of the way. Not as much air is needed to enhance the bouquet of most white wines.

- When dining at an appetizer buffet, place the items you want to eat on your plate, including salsas, dips, and so forth, then begin eating. **Never eat directly from the serving tray**.

A social *faux pas* may turn off your friends, but business missteps can be deal-killers. The pitfalls are endless. An American tourist abroad is conspicuous—an American on business abroad is even more conspicuous. Every step is analyzed and every moment is filled with seeming significance. To avoid making a global goof, keep in mind the following tips when it comes to business travel and communication around the world.

International travel
Arab countries

- Do not use your left hand to hold, offer, or receive materials; Arabs use the left hand to touch toilet paper and for bodily hygiene. Instead, use your right hand: eat with it, present gifts with it, and touch with it. If you must write with your left hand, apologize for doing so.

- Avoid showing the sole of the shoe or inadvertently pointing it at someone. The shoe soles are the lowest and dirtiest part of the body—it's rude to point them at someone.

- Long, direct eye contact among men is important. In fact, staring is not considered rude or impolite.

- Never use curse words or mention God.

- Public displays of affection are frowned upon.

- Keep household pets away from visiting Arabs. Most Arabs do not like to be touched by or be in the presence of such pets, especially dogs.

China

- Do not refuse tea during a business discussion. Instead, always drink it, even if you are offered a dozen cups a day.

- Business cards are often exchanged, and yours should be printed in your own *and* the Chinese language. Also, it is more respectful to present your card—or a gift or any other article—using both hands. Study their card; don't just stick it in your pocket.

- Hugging and kissing when greeting are uncommon.

- Posture is important, so don't slouch or put your feet on desks or chairs.

- Personal space is less in China. The Chinese stand much closer, invading *your space* without realizing it.

- Don't begin eating until the host picks up his or her chopsticks.

- Before taking any photographs of local people, ask their permission.

France

- A light, quick, single handshake happens quite frequently. A strong, pumping handshake is considered uncultured.

- Do not schedule a breakfast meeting. (The French read the paper at *le petit dejeuner.*) Instead, meet after 10 A.M.

- To call a taxi, many Parisians simply snap their fingers.

- When seated, the French customarily cross the legs at the knees. Good posture and decorum are virtues in France.

- Always use a tissue or handkerchief when sneezing, and be as discreet as possible when blowing your nose.

- The French find it strange to pick up sandwiches and other such foods with the fingers. It is more common to cut them with a knife and fork.

Germany

- Do not address a business associate by his or her first name, even if you've known each other for years. Instead, wait for an invitation to do so.

- Never open a closed door without knocking first.

- Chewing gum while conversing with another person is considered rude.

- Men rise when a woman enters the room or when conversing with a woman. However, women may remain seated.

- Never call a German at home on business and most certainly not in the evening.

- Handsome desk accessories make welcome gifts. Do not bring gifts lavished with your corporate logo.

Japan

- Do not bring up business on the golf course. Instead, wait for your host to take the initiative.

- If you really want to please your Japanese colleagues, greet them with a bow and a smile.

- Displaying an open mouth is considered rude in Japan. That is one reason many Japanese, especially the women, cover their mouths when giggling or laughing.

- Crossing the legs at the knees or ankles is the preferred form rather than with one ankle over the other knee.

- Blowing your nose in public is considered rude.

- As an international guest, the Japanese will expect you to precede them walking down a hall or entering a room, elevator, automobile, and so forth.

Mexico

- Do not send a bouquet of red or yellow flowers as a gift. (Those colors are associated with evil spirits and death.) Instead, send a premium box of chocolates.

- While eating, both hands should be kept above the table, not in the lap.

- In public, men should not stand with their hands in their pockets.

- If a man stands with his hands on his hips, it signals hostility or challenge.

- Bargaining in stores is natural and expected.

- **Never** visit churches or religious sites while wearing short-shorts, tank tops, cut-off shirts, or shorts.

- Nude bathing is very offensive to Mexicans.

When making a presentation to foreigners, do not use American acronyms or slang. Few Germans, for example, would know what a Catch-22 is or what ASAP means. Do your homework. If you are leaving the country, buy a book and study the different cultures. Hire an intercultural trainer to educate you on foreign etiquette. Hone your global communication techniques and you will be successful. Establishing an atmosphere of trust and compatibility—which takes time for impatient Americans—is a learned art. If people are comfortable with us, our presence at any event will be valued.

CHAPTER 12

Self-Promotion; "Blowing Your Horn"

Self-promotion need not be reserved for public relations experts or high-profile government officials. Everyone in the business arena should go out of their way to make sure they are recognized and noticed. Most people are naive and think their track record should speak for itself, which in many cases, it does not. You must to be able to "blow your horn" while climbing the corporate ladder of success.

One way to increase your chances of success is to keep a journal or file of all of your accomplishments throughout the past year. Make copies of memos, letters of congratulation, ideas you have suggested that have been implemented, problems you have solved, and so forth. When it's time for your annual review, you have the information you need at your fingertips. Make a list, summarizing all you have done for the past twelve months. Put together a brief, one-page synopsis to be passed on to your manager. Don't worry about sounding conceited—this makes his or her job easier and at the same time serves as a reminder why you are such a valuable employee. Update your resume each year and keep a copy in **your** file. You never know when an opportunity may come your way. If it does, you'll be prepared.

Another way to increase your chances of success is to volunteer to speak or present as often as possible. Yes, public speaking is the number one fear—over death, over flying, over snakes and spiders. But, the more you do it, the better you'll become and the easier it will be to do. Practice your information aloud. Rehearse. Listen to yourself on a cassette recorder. You'll be surprised at how you may even start to enjoy it. This provides you with the exposure and recognition not usually afforded to a person who sits in the background, quietly doing his or her job.

No matter where you live, there are dozens of clubs and organizations that use outside speakers on a regular basis. Become active in your professional organizations and other business groups. Holding a part-time political position is another effective way to increase your name recognition while contributing to your community. Get involved with volunteer work. Speak at the PTA, United Way, March of Dimes, or any type of fund raiser. When you chair a committee, make sure your name is listed on the program along with the other committee members. You'll feel better about yourself and you increase your chances of being noticed, which could lead to more opportunities.

If you are unable at the last minute to make a presentation and a colleague must deliver it for you, make sure you get a list of who will be attending the meeting. Prior to your departure, put together a brief overview using bulleted words and phrases pertaining to your presentation; **with your name on it**, send it to everyone who will be at the meeting. This allows you to make certain that credit is given where it is due. Your colleague may not deliberately forget to mention your name, but why take the chance?

Follow-up all important conversations with a brief memo recapping what was discussed. Attach copies of relevant information to the memo. When you have done a particularly good job with a project for a client, ask for a letter acknowledging that fact. Send a copy to your boss and/or the CEO. Make sure a copy goes into **your** file.

Your office makes a strong statement *about you* and *how you* want to be perceived by others. Well-placed plaques, tasteful gifts of recognition, or signed autographs to you can be positive additions. Framed pictures of your family and friends add warmth.

Top people initiate. They have the courage to take chances, disagree, risk failure for a chance at success, challenge policies, make unpopular decisions, and speak up. They are not afraid to stand up for and be passionate about what they believe in. Are you that type of person? In the future, make a conscious effort to become more assertive during meetings. Don't allow someone else to imply that *your* idea was *their* idea. You know the old saying, "No risk, no gain." It's true. By never taking any risks, you have nothing to fear but also nothing to gain. The next time you are *thinking about* sharing an idea but are afraid, take the plunge. What's the worst that can happen? Analyze the potential benefits of taking a risk; take a clear look at what might possibly go wrong and what consequences you would suffer if the risk proved too great. Growth always involves the risk of possible loss but refusing to grow involves an even greater risk. Work on taking calculated risks—you'll be pleased with yourself and glad you took the risk. Again, it's an excellent way to get noticed.

When you are facilitating a meeting, provide a broad outline of your agenda and what subjects will be covered. Be flexible with the order of the discussion. It is more important to be able to read your audience than to be so structured it stifles creativity and candor. Start with the most important idea or issue and work backward. When you save the most important item for last, you risk running out of time. Keep the meeting on track; do not allow anyone to ramble or go off on tangents. Stay focused and **lead** the meeting; this boosts credibility with colleagues. Whether you are facilitating, presenting, or attending as a participant, bring copies of your agenda or outline. When appropriate, send a copy to each person prior to the meeting. Own the setting: If you want authority and a no-nonsense atmosphere, schedule your meeting in the boardroom. If you want an equal, on-target exchange, look for a conference table in neutral territory. Whatever your choice, be comfortable with and *own* the surroundings.

Whenever you go into a meeting with a new idea or proposal, summarize it in outline form on paper. Put your name at the top of the page. Make enough copies to distribute to everyone at the meeting and place them face down in front of you. Pitch the idea. If it bombs, leave the papers where they are. If your idea goes over well, pass them out by saying, "I've got the key points in writing. Let's build on this together."

Speak up at least once during every meeting you attend. Studies show that people who talk more in conversations with peers, friends and strangers are perceived as leaders. Speak up to increase your visibility. It also lets the group know you are listening.

Another way to increase your visibility and chances of success is to remember to write a follow-up note or congratulatory letter whenever possible and appropriate. This is an incredibly valuable way to establish your professional presence because so few people take the time to do it. If you attend a seminar or convention, get invited to a holiday party, or are given complimentary tickets to a concert from the company, send a note. You are distinguishing yourself from others while increasing your chances of success.

Newspaper clippings relating to a client or colleague can be sent on a regular basis. Include a brief note saying you were "thinking of them" or "remembered your recent conversation" on the enclosed topic. This is an excellent way to extend your mutual interest.

Make business referrals to clients and colleagues whenever possible. When I am asked to train a program that is not my area of expertise, I refer the business to a competitor or do cross-referrals with individuals I respect. Your willingness and ability to do this sets you apart from those in your field who come across as territorial and insecure. Whenever possible, *help someone else out*—it can come back to you tenfold.

Volunteer to write a column or an article for your company newsletter or put together your own one page newsletter every four to six weeks. Address relevant issues, ideas, and areas to strengthen the company, your division, specific jobs, and so forth.

It's a great way to become more visible within your organization. Have extra copies printed to pass on to your manager and colleagues. Put a copy into **your** file. Self-promotion through volunteerism and initiative makes you a more valuable employee and provides you with greater esteem in the eyes of your manager and colleagues.

Write a one-page informational piece or newsletter you can mail to potential and current clients. Make sure it is on company letterhead with your name printed somewhere on the copy. Send a copy to your manager. Put a copy into **your** file.

The art of self-promotion does not mean you have to become pushy and obnoxious. There is no need to boast and brag. Your goal is to bring positive attention to yourself and develop a reputation as someone who is willing to take some chances.

Whether you are standing in front of a group speaking, writing a newsletter, or volunteering for a special project, you enhance your total image by taking the initiative and receiving credit for your professional accomplishments. Live your life to the fullest and reach for the farthest limits of your potential. Put these suggestions to use and within one year you will be amazed at the changes in *your* professional image and *your* overall personal communication style. Most importantly, the way you are perceived by others will dramatically improve. The opportunities to utilize and maximize your potential are limitless.

CHAPTER 13

Making Great Presentations

Whether we express an idea at a meeting, sell a product or service, have a discussion with our spouse over finances, ask our boss for a raise, converse with friends about politics, or try to persuade the butcher to slice us that special cut of meat, we are presenting. It makes no difference whether we speak to one person we know or to one thousand we don't—*a presentation is a presentation is a presentation*. Of our wants, needs, ideas, and most important, of *our self*. Whatever we do, wherever we work, a key part of our job is to persuade other people to a course of action we would like them to take. We're talking about *your personal impact* and *your ability* to connect with others whenever you have something to say.

In order to give a powerful, effective presentation, it's essential to think about more than just yourself and your material—you must first consider your audience. Ultimately, the success of any presentation can only be measured from the audience's perspective. Although this is simple, common sense, many of us get so caught up in our own material or nervousness we forget to think about the audience.

● Many speakers *assume* the audience is hanging on each and every word, soaking up the information like sponges; research has proven they are not. The audience is drifting in and out during a presentation—thinking about other issues at work, concerns about what is happening in their personal lives, or how much fun they will be having while on vacation next week. The attention span of an average individual is thirty seconds.

Most presentations are persuasive-informative. We usually have a reason *why* we are speaking to a particular audience. What's in it for your audience members to be listening to you present your information to them? What outcome are you looking for after presenting this information to them? Write down in a single sentence relating to what you want your audience to *know* and *do* as a result of your presentation. Have a clear-cut objective. Remember your success depends upon your audience and how well they can relate to your information. Delivering a positive statement that contains a benefit to your audience will keep them interested and remind them *why* they are there listening to you.

The next step is to think of as many open-ended questions as you can beginning with who, what, where, when, why, and how. Each question relates directly to the clear-cut single sentence/objective you have just developed. (Stay away from rhetorical questions or questions needing a yes, no or single-word response.) Each question you thought of can become a point of information or issue to be addressed while you are speaking to your audience. Write down all of the questions and answer them in detail. This step also helps you to prepare for answering questions you may be asked while you're presenting your information.

As you move in and out of your points of information, occasionally repeat the single, clear-cut objective you developed (to your listeners). This subtly reminds them of what's in it for them to be listening to your presentation. It helps keep *you* on track and continually pulls your audience back into your presentation—in the event that they were day dreaming or not paying attention. (As mentioned earlier, retention is approximately 5 percent.) This is an easy formula to learn and will enable you to become more comfortable when presenting any and all types of information.

Introductions and conclusions

You may want to add an introduction and conclusion to your presentation. Think about three elements your presentation has in common, or three elements your audience has in common. Develop three sentences to make up a bold, dynamic introduction to grab your listeners' attention. Each sentence can begin with the same word or group of words. For example: "Did you know...? Did you know...? Did you know...?" or "In the 1970s, we did it this way.... In the 1980s, we did it this way.... In the 1990s, we did it this way...." Share three facts with your audience they may not have known. This enhances your rhythm at the beginning of your presentation.

Persuasive people have always known the power of a trio of ideas. Consider these three-beat advertising slogans: *The few, the proud, the Marines. Reduce, reuse, recycle.* There are also three-step commands: *"Lights! Camera! Action!" "Ready! Aim! Fire!" "On your mark! Get set! Go!"* At See's Candies, a store known for its fine chocolates, workers operate by the three S's of *smiles, service,* and *samples.* Employees of Domino's Pizza know that their jobs revolve around FFF: *fast, friendly, free delivery.* Target's motto is *fast, friendly, and fun.* By recognizing the appeal of three, you can increase the persuasiveness of your presentation.

Use analogies or story telling with vivid, visual imagery people can enjoy. Listeners will remember a story and the details told in your introduction (or during your presentation) before they will remember statistics quoted or technical details provided. Draw from your own experiences, start a personal story collection, and use humor.

This method can also be used at the end of your presentation or when you are concluding your speech. You would use the same concept and theory, just change your three count rhythmic ending/conclusion to tie everything together. Your closing does not have to be similar to your opening/introduction. You can end your presentation with an overall summary of your information or choose three of the most important elements of your information and reiterate them during your conclusion.

When you are ready to formulate your presentation, type it on your computer. Type the speech on the upper two-thirds of each page, double-spacing between lines, and sextuple-spacing between paragraphs. With that spacing, there is less chance of losing your place and your eyes are never forced to the bottom of the page, making you look too far down and away from the audience. This helps you maintain eye contact. Use an 18- or 20-point bold type, upper and lower case. Print the speech on off-white, matte-finish, porous paper in the event there is overhead lighting, which can create a glare and it difficult to read. Be sure you number the pages in case they get out of order when you are practicing. **Never** flip the pages, (unless they are in a three-ring notebook), so they're upside down. When you finish a page, just slide it to the side, face up. That way the audience does not become overly aware or distracted by your pages.

When speaking for longer periods of time, and you have a sizable amount of information to deliver, consider using a three-ring notebook for your presentation. (For example, if you are the facilitator of a full-day training session.) Slide each page of your presentation into a three-hole punched clear protector page. The pages turn more smoothly; if you're giving the same presentation numerous times, it stays in excellent shape. You can also tab the different areas or points of your speech, allowing additional freedom and flexibility when moving from point-to-point.

Self-talk

Think about your behavior and the way you talk to yourself, especially when you are presenting important information. Most people say negative things. They constantly tell themselves they are not good enough or smart enough. They tell themselves how stupid they are or they forgot this or forgot that. They do it so often, they begin to believe it. Negative thoughts create self-destructive energy. A constant barrage of verbal self-abuse and negative self-talk does a lot of damage to others' perceptions of you. This can cost you a great deal in both personal and business relationships.

Most important, it can affect you when you are delivering an important presentation.

Negative self-talk allows people to see things about us that are not there. We tend to see and hear what other people tell us about themselves, and who knows better than they do? Think about this the next time you are putting yourself down in front of another person. This habit usually stems from the conditioning we received in our society as children. How many times were you told to stop being a showoff or were ignored as you paraded around in a new outfit? You do not have to tell everyone how great you are but do not talk negatively about or to yourself either. If you must talk to yourself, say positive affirmations—remind yourself to breathe. Eliminate the people in your life who are not positive or who say snide remarks to you.

When speaking in front of a large group, many presenters look for and seek out positive strokes and encouraging feedback. A search for the nods of approval, smiles of appreciation, thumbs up, or a standing ovation can negatively effect delivery. Be realistic. Interaction with your audience is good, but allowing their reaction to your information affect the way you present it can be deadly. If you make a mistake, don't beat yourself up or roll your eyes toward the ceiling. Many times your audience wasn't paying attention anyway, so all you have done was to draw (negative) attention to yourself. Let it go and continue on.

As mentioned earlier, if you must say anything, say "excuse me." **Never** apologize or say you're "sorry" when you do make a mistake; this takes away from your credibility, believability, and authority.

Whenever possible and appropriate, say "I believe" rather than "I think" when speaking. This verbiage is more forceful, powerful, and convincing. Your listeners will buy into your idea, plan, proposal, project, and so forth more readily when you speak with passion and sound as if you believe what you are saying as well. If you are not sure or are at all hesitant about your information, say "I think."

You are the message

In *You Are the Message* by Roger Ailes, he talks about the one secret we need to know to succeed: "You are the message." This has been my philosophy for as long as I can remember, so I wholeheartedly agree with him. When you're not having a great day (or if you've been up all night with a new baby, worked into the wee hours on your business presentation, or fear you may be about to lose your job), your audience doesn't care. They **want** you to do a good job, they **expect** you to do a good job, and **you can do** a good job!

Move into what is considered the *actor role. Play the part of the person you know yourself to be on your best day.* **You are the message** and want to appear as if you are in complete control, totally focused, and self-confident. Although you may not feel 100 percent, (especially when **you are** having a bad day), your audience does not know how you're feeling. What you're feeling internally is generally not what you're projecting externally. You appear more calm and relaxed. Use this knowledge to your advantage to increase your self-confidence. By *appearing* confident, people will *believe* you to be confident. The trick in good communications is to be consistently *you*, at your best, in all situations. Nobody can play *you* as well as you can.

In our communication seminars, we do extensive videotaping. Ninety percent of the time, participants admit they *appear calmer than they were feeling.* Videotape yourself when speaking, presenting, or practicing. You immediately benefit from hearing and seeing what's happening with your external image. Once you get past the initial shock reaction, the opportunity for self-awareness and self-improvement is tremendous.

Effective use of visual aids

Studies by the University of Minnesota and the 3M Corporation along with the Wharton School revealed that if you stand up and give a presentation using visual aids, your audience, client, or prospect is *43 percent more likely to be persuaded* than by using words alone. From the same study: If you stand up and give a presentation, your customer, client, or prospect is willing to pay **26 percent more money** for the same product or service.

Additional reasons why visual aids should be used when you speak:

- Group consensus occurs **21 percent more often** in meetings with visuals than without.

- The time required to present a concept can be **reduced up to 40 percent** with the use of visuals.

- When visuals were used in teaching a course on vocabulary, **learning improved 200 percent!**

Here is some important information to consider when adding visual aids to your presentation for the most positive impact:

- Use a maximum of six to eight words per line, six to eight lines of information per page. Use bulleted words only—not complete sentences. Your audience isn't stupid; they can read. As you move to each bullet, provide details, examples, explanations, and specifics.

- When using transparencies, do not play "peek-a-boo" by sliding your paper down the page, uncovering information as you go. I watched the president of a large corporation stand up, rip the paper (covering information) from the presenter's visuals, and scream, "We are not complete morons!" (The poor fellow was so traumatized by this outburst, he hasn't presented since.)

- The psychological sight line of your audience is from left to right; **you** should be first and foremost—your visual aid is secondary. (Think about when you're reading a book.) As a presenter, keep flip charts, computer screens, slides, videos, easels, graphs, overheads, and so forth **to your left.**

- Ask yourself the following questions: "Can my audience quickly and easily grasp what they see? Is each visual truly enhancing my presentation or am I hiding behind it, using it as a crutch?" Answer honestly—you must appear credible and believable.

- Keep your visual aids clean, clear, and simple. Remember to touch, turn, and talk; do not have your back to your audience when speaking. Work from a hard copy of your notes; do not talk to (or read from) the wall.

- Don't forget actual objects—the best visual aid is the *real thing*. Pictures are another option to consider. Get as many as you can—have someone else pass them out for you so you're not distracted **or** wait and pass the item at the end of your presentation.

- Do not darken a room to the point where you cannot see your audience's eyes—*dim the lights*.

- No more than three curves on a graph; one or two are most effective.

- Use color, but no more than three primary colors: Red, blue, green, purple, yellow. Remember that for anyone who is color-blind, green may be seen as brown.

- Translate complex numbers into pie charts or bar graphs; use overlays for complex points or financial information. Use a handout if the information is too "busy."

- Do not play with collapsible pointers, markers, pens, and so forth. This can be **very** distracting.

- Check your equipment before beginning your presentation. Have a backup in the event your computer or machine breaks down during your presentation. With a small group, a tabletop easel notebook works well as a backup.

- Always insist on getting into the room where you will be presenting **prior to speaking.** If you are presenting to a large group at a hotel, arrive the night before and read through your entire presentation **at least twice, aloud**, in the room where you will be presenting. You will be much more comfortable and relaxed the next day when it's your turn to speak.

Delivering your presentation

Once you have your presentation written and your visual aids ready, the next step is to **deliver it aloud** numerous times. Many presenters don't take the time to practice. They simply "wing it." This type of speaker usually rambles and goes off on tangents, boring his or her audience to tears. If it's only a five- to ten-minute presentation, I strongly recommend **practicing it aloud a minimum of fifteen to twenty times**. This allows you to become accustomed to the rhythm, timing, and feel of your message. (While George Bush was president, he used to practice for up to eighteen hours a day when preparing for a presidential address.)

Standing in front of a mirror enables you to become aware of your gestures. Be natural with them, not forced and rigid. Practice with any audiovisual aids or props you intend to use. After you have rehearsed your information and feel comfortable with the delivery, tape record yourself. Listen to the cassette in your car during your drive to and from work, in the evening at home, or on the weekend. Videotape your presentation. Play the tape and observe the way your posture and gestures relate to your message. Pay special attention to the magnitude of your voice and the overall coherence and flow of your information.

If you will be delivering your presentation from behind a lectern, make sure you have practiced it from there. Bear in mind the lectern creates a physical barrier between you and your audience. (It's usually used for more formal presentations.) If possible, get out from behind the lectern so you can gesture with your hands and arms. However, if there is a stationery mike, you will not have the ability to *walk and talk* during your presentation. Before your audience arrives, check the height of the lectern—many are adjustable. Double-check the audio being used for the microphone; find out if someone will be available to adjust the sound while you are speaking, if necessary. A hand-held microphone or a "lavaliere" mike, which hangs around the neck or clips on to the lapel, is an option to consider when presenting less formally. The latter offers extra freedom to move out from behind the lectern and also frees up the arms and hands for more gestures. (Be careful not to trip over any of the cords.) Another type of microphone is a "remote" mike. It is a cordless, battery-operated microphone with a miniature microphone that clips to the tie, blouse, or coat lapel with a wire leading to a portable power pack that clips to the waist, usually at your back, under a coat or jacket. (This is the type of microphone I use when presenting to large groups.)

While you are being introduced, smile at the person who is introducing you and/or smile at your audience. (Many presenters don't know *what* to do during this time, making them appear uncomfortable before he or she even begins to speak.) After you have been introduced, thank the person who introduced you (use his or her name) and walk deliberately, enthusiastically, and purposefully to the lectern.

Effective communications checklist

Use the following checklist to help evaluate how you are communicating. As you look at and listen to yourself, keep in mind you do not have much time to impress your audience. If you do not persuade your listeners within a couple of minutes, they will probably tune you out.

1. When you speak, do you look and sound energetic? Enthusiastic? Excited? Do you speak with conviction and passion? *Energy can make up for distractions.*

2. Do you have a warm, open smile? *A smile shows not only on your mouth but in and around your eyes; it demonstrates openness and likability.*

3. Do you have a clear, concise beginning/introduction that hooks listeners and makes them want to listen? *With little time to waste, most listeners resent waiting for you to get to the point.*

4. Do you speak only when you are looking into someone's eyes and finish your thought with them before you move on? *Eye contact helps you connect with your listeners on a more personal level, making you persuasive and credible.*

5. Do you vary the tone and volume of your voice? Your speech patterns? *Both help to keep listeners interested and awake. Skilled presenters, comfortable using their voices to make a point, intentionally lower their voices to make their audience strain to hear them.*

6. Do you avoid *fillers and non-words*, using pauses and silence instead?

7. Have you eliminated complicated and technical jargon? *Have you simplified your information so everyone, including yourself, understands it?*

8. Do you use stories and examples to illustrate and support the points you are making? *Personal tidbits of information people can relate to are the most memorable.*

9. Is your body language confident: head up, shoulders back, weight evenly balanced on your feet, hands free to gesture and in sync with your message? *Your goal is to become a natural communicator.*

10. Is what you have to say more interesting than your overall physical appearance? Are your listeners distracted by your unkempt hair, dirty nails, unpolished shoes? *You can more easily make positive changes in your dress and appearance than any other skill, thus gain immediate benefit.*

11. Do you think about your listeners before you speak to them so you can prioritize what *you* have to say according to what *they* want to hear? *Listeners may not hear you until you speak about what's important to them. Remember to have a key message for your audience.*

12. Do you stay on the topic? *The principal of MEGO (my eyes glaze over) sets in after about three minutes. Speak directly and concisely without rambling or going off on tangents.*

13. Do your listeners know what you want them to do next: arrange a follow-up meeting, sign an agreement, make an introduction? *Make it succinct and clear.*

14. Do you look, sound, and act like someone you would like to do business with? *If you are not comfortable with what you see, it's likely that others will not be comfortable either. Practice, practice, practice your information.*

Times have changed in corporate America. It used to be the most qualified person got the job. Today, in a situation where three people with equal qualifications are interviewed for a job, the one with the best communication skills gets it. This becomes a bigger consideration every year. Taking the time to understand your communication style along with the knowledge of proper use of body language will enable you to become a more effective, dynamic, and promotable communicator. If you look, sound, and act like someone you would like to do business with, others will too.

Some final words of advice: When you speak, to one or hundreds, don't fall prey to the words of Ralph Waldo Emerson: "What you are speaks so loud I cannot hear what you say." To be a good coach for yourself and a comfortable, confident speaker, raise your awareness of how you are communicating. Practice the tools and techniques of effective communications daily—in meetings, conversations, and phone calls. Give yourself feedback *after you speak* to reinforce what is working for you, then single out specific areas still needing enhancement. Look for opportunities to present so you can continue to cultivate the skills you need to get your message—and your personality—across most effectively. Whatever your situation, become comfortable with all aspects of your presentation and master the delivery. Perform as *you*, when *you* are at your best. Know you are reaching people and making yourself more successful in every facet of your life. **You will then realize you have become a persuasive, powerful, and dynamic communicator.**

BIBLIOGRAPHY

Adler, Mortimer J. *How to Speak How to Listen*. New York: Macmillan Publishing, 1983.

Ailes, Roger with Jon Kraushar. *You Are the Message*. New York: Doubleday, 1988.

Axtell, Roger E. *Gestures*. New York: John Wiley and Sons, 1991.

Baldridge, Letticia. *Complete Guide to Executive Manners*. New York: Rawson Associates, 1985.

Benton, D.A. *Lions Don't Need to Roar*. New York: Warner Books, 1992.

Bixler, Susan. *Professional Presence*. New York: Putnam, 1991.

Bixler, Susan and Nancy Nix-Rice. *The New Professional Image*. CITY: Adams Media, 1997.

Brinkman, Dr. Rick and Dr. Rick Kirschner. *Dealing With People You Can't Stand*. New York: McGraw-Hill, 1994.

Brown, Lillian. *Your Public Best*. New York: NewMarket Press, 1989.

Craig, Betty. *Don't Slurp Your Soup*. New Brighton, MN: Brighton Publications, 1992.

Decker, Bert. *You've Got to Be Believed to Be Heard*. New York: St. Martins Press, 1992.

Dimitrius, Jo-Ellan, Ph.D., and Mark Mazzarella. *Reading People*. New York: Random House, Inc., 1998.

DuPont, M. Kay. *Business Etiquette and Professionalism*. Menlo Park, CA: Crisp Publications, 1990.

Fast, Julius. *Body Language in the Workplace*. New York: Penguin Books, 1994.

Feldman, Sandor S. *Mannerisms of Speech and Gestures*. New York: International Universities Press, Inc., 1959.

Frank, Milo. *How to Get Your Point Across in 30 Seconds or Less*. New York: Pocket Books, 1986.

Gelb, Michael J. *Present Yourself!* Torrance, CA: Jalmar Press, 1988.

Glaser, Connie Brown and Barbara Steinberg Smalley. *More Power to You!* New York: Warner Books, 1992.

Glass, Lillian, Ph.D. *Talk to Win.* CITY: Perigee Books, 1987.

Gray, James Jr. *The Winning Image.* New York: Amacon, 1982.

Jordan, Nick. *The Face of Feeling. Psychology Today* 20, no. 1 (January 1986) p. 8.

Linver, Sandy. *SpeakEasy.* New York: Summit Books, 1978.

Mandell, Terri. *Power Schmoozing.* Los Angeles: First House Press, 1993.

Manhard, Stephen J. *The Goof-Proofer.* New York: Macmillan Publishing, 1985.

Mehrabian, Albert. *Nonverbal Communication.* Chicago: Aldine-Atherton, 1972.

Murphy, Kevin J. *Effective Listening.* Salem, NH: ELI Press, 1992.

Peoples, David A. *Presentations Plus.* New York: John Wiley and Sons, 1992.

Rafe, Stephen C. *How to Be Prepared to Think on Your Feet.* New York: HarperBusiness, 1990.

RoAne, Susan. *How To Work A Room.* New York: Warner Books, 1988.

Sabath, Ann Marie. *Business Etiquette in Brief.* Holbrook, MA: Bob Adams, Inc., 1993.

Schloff, Laurie and Marcia Yudkin. *Smart Speaking.* New York: Penguin Books, 1992.

Seitz, Victoria A. *Your Executive Image.* Holbrook, MA: Bob Adams, Inc., 1992.

Stone, Janet and Jane Bachner. *Speaking Up.* New York: Carroll and Graff Publishers/Richard Gallen edition, 1994.

Van Ekeren, Glenn. *Speakers Sourcebook II.* Englewood Cliffs, NJ: Prentice Hall, 1994.

Wainwright, Gordon R. *Body Language.* Chicago, IL: NTC Publishing Group, 1985.

Walters, Lilly. *Secrets Of Successful Speakers.* New York: McGraw Hill, 1993.

ABOUT THE AUTHOR

KATHRYN J. VOLIN, founder and president of the Minneapolis, Minnesota consulting firm Communication Concepts International, Inc., (CCII) is one of the nation's leading experts on verbal, nonverbal, and written communications in business.

Her business career in corporate communications training, speech preparation, sales, marketing, management, leadership, image enhancement, style, and public speaking/platform skills spans more than twenty years. This background has given her the ability to professionally guide and advise her clients while providing results-oriented, highly relevant, constructive coaching. Her unique and innovative solutions to communication obstacles are consistently rated to be exceptional and unequaled.

Kathryn's local, national, and international communication training and experience along with continual support and coaching is what makes her and CCII one of the most recommended training resources in the industry. CCII's Effective Communications Program and executive coaching sessions are considered by many major corporations to be an essential part of their executive training process.

Clients include: 3M, Alliant Techsystems, Amoco, Anheuser-Busch, Avery Dennison, Baltimore Gas and Electric, Cargill, Chrysler Corporation, Dayton Hudson Corporation, DynaMark, Ernst & Young, First Banks, Ford Motor Company, FannieMae, H.B. Fuller Company, Imation Corporation, Medtronic, Merrill Corporation, Mervyn's

California, Nestle, Nordstroms, Northern States Power, Norstan, Pillsbury, Service Merchandise, SUPERVALU, St. Paul Companies, Target Stores, and U.S. Bancorp.

Her mission is simple: to make sure each and every individual she works with recognizes and capitalizes on his or her own personal communication style, qualities, and assets. At the same time, she strives to impart a thorough understanding of the techniques that can be used to immediately, positively, and profoundly impact their overall image and the way they are perceived. The result: a confident, persuasive, *buffed and polished* communicator prepared to master the challenges of today's competitive business environment.

For more information about Communication Concepts International, Inc., please call (612) 851-9697; fax line (612) 851-9692. To ensure a prompt reply to your fax, please include your name, company name, address, telephone number, fax number, and the nature of your inquiry.

Give the Gift of
Buff and Polish
to Your Friends and Colleagues

CHECK YOUR LEADING BOOKSTORE OR ORDER HERE

❑ **YES**, I want _____ copies of *Buff and Polish* at $12.95 each, plus $3 shipping per book (Minnesota residents please add 84¢ sales tax per book). Canadian orders must be accompanied by a postal money order in U.S. funds. Allow 15 days for delivery.

My check or money order for $_____ is enclosed.
Please charge my ❑ Visa ❑ MasterCard

Name _____

Organization _____

Address _____

City/State/Zip _____

Phone _____

Card # _____Exp. Date _____

Signature _____

Please make your check payable and return to:

Pentagon Publishing
2626 East 82nd Street; Suite 228
Minneapolis, MN 55425-1381

Fax or call your credit card order to: 651-436-1212